NORMANDY JUNE 1944

THE NIGHT OF LIBERATION

Text **Gilles Vallée**
Illustrations **Christophe Esquerré**
Colour **Paul Gros**

HEIMDAL

To Xavier, Pierre-Edouard, Charles and Marie, who are the youth of today.
To my wife, Claire, for her patience.
To my family.

Gilles Vallée

For Melissa, my goddaughter.
To my French and Canadian family.

Christophe Esquerré

To Jean Vervalle member of the Airborne Museum and specialist in the history of the C- 47 who died before the publication of this book, which he was waiting for with enthusiasm and curiosity.

To Karl Leisner, interned in the camp at Dachau. Ordained a priest right under the nose of his captors, he was liberated by the Americans. Here are the last lines of his diary: "Bless also, O Lord, my enemies!"

Text: Gilles Vallée
Illustrations: Christophe Esquerré
Colour: Paul Gros
Project-Coordinator: Jean-Charles Stasi
Graphic work and layout: Paul Gros
Translation: Iona Singh

Éditions Heimdal
BP 61350 - 14406 BAYEUX Cedex
Tel: 02.31.51.68.68   Fax: 02.31.51.68.60
E-mail: Editions.Heimdal@wanadoo.fr
www.editions-heimdal.fr

Front Cover: June 4, 1944, Exeter Aerodrome, England, Bill Atlee boarding the C-47 Lady Lillian.

INTRODUCTION

Colonel Frank X. Krebs in his office.

Robert Lee Wolverton and Frank Xavier Krebs

Colonel Robert Lee Wolverton was Commander of the 3rd Battalion of the 506th Regiment of the 101st Airborne Division (101st Airborne). Born in 1914, he became a cadet at the Military Academy at West Point, he was much loved by his men. In the early hours of June 6, 1944 he was shot in his parachute harness even before touching the Normandy soil that he was coming to liberate, without the chance to defend himself. He was not yet 30 years old.

On D-Day, Colonel Frank Xavier Krebs was piloting the command plane of the 440th Troop Carrier Group in which Wolverton and his team had taken their places. Colonel Krebs and his co-pilot, Major Howard Cannon, flew together until the end of the war, participating in all the major air missions in Europe. Always called "Colonel" by members of the 440th throughout the years after the war, he retired from the U.S. Air Force after a long career. He died at his home in Accokeek, near Washington, at the age of 89 years.

Two men engaged in the same tragic events. And yet the destiny of each was so different.

Here is their story and that of the men who climbed into the *Stoy Hora* C-47 airplane along with them, in what was to become the historic night of the 5 to 6 June 1944.

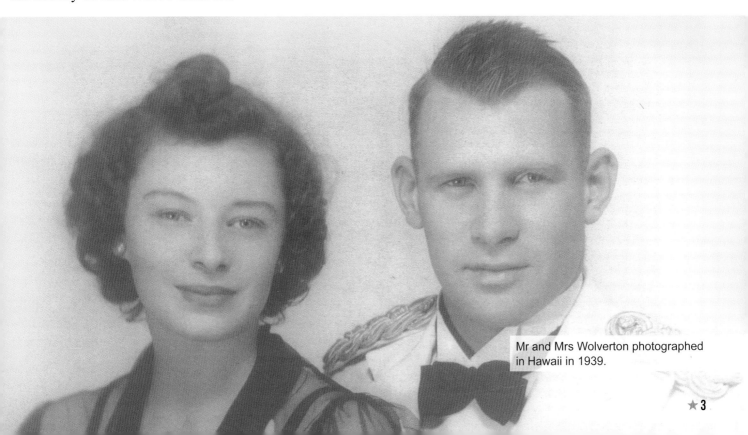

Mr and Mrs Wolverton photographed in Hawaii in 1939.

In 1940, when Hitler was ready to invade Britain, the British Prime Minister Winston Churchill declared : "The Battle of Britain is about to begin. Upon this battle depends the survival of Christian civilisation."

Eisenhower and paratroopers from the 502nd Parachute Infantry Regiment of the 101st Airborne Division, England, June 5, 1944.

Four years later, the course of events had now changed. The invading armies were no longer the same. In the run-up to D-Day, the Allied commanders were always invoking God. The senior officers were fully aware that the lives of many young men placed under their command would depend on their decisions. Their responsibilities in the merciless fight against Nazism was overwhelming. Forecast losses for U.S. airborne troops were alarming. The Supreme Commander of the Allied Expeditionary Forces, General Dwight David Eisenhower, nicknamed "Ike", was anxious. With the sentiment that he would send many of them to their death, he decided to pay a visit to the men of the 502nd PIR of the 101st Airborne Division on the afternoon of June 5.

Lieutenant Bobuck's group, who were at another aerodrome at the time, did not have the chance to exchange a few words with Ike. So shortly before the flight for Normandy, while the war correspondent Ward Smith was boarding the C-47 *Stoy Hora*, Major Cannon (copilot) read out loud the message of encouragement from Eisenhower.

SUPREME HEADQUARTERS
ALLIED EXPEDITIONARY FORCE

Soldiers, Sailors and Airmen of the Allied Expeditionary Force!

You are about to embark upon the Great Crusade, toward which we have striven these many months. The eyes of the world are upon you. The hopes and prayers of liberty-loving people everywhere march with you. In company with our brave Allies and brothers-in-arms on other Fronts, you will bring about the destruction of the German war machine, the elimination of Nazi tyranny over the oppressed peoples of Europe, and security for ourselves in a free world.

Your task will not be an easy one. Your enemy is well trained, well equipped and battle-hardened. He will fight savagely.

But this is the year 1944! Much has happened since the Nazi triumphs of 1940-41. The United Nations have inflicted upon the Germans great defeats, in open battle, man-to-man. Our air offensive has seriously reduced their strength in the air and their capacity to wage war on the ground. Our Home Fronts have given us an overwhelming superiority in weapons and munitions of war, and placed at our disposal great reserves of trained fighting men. The tide has turned! The free men of the world are marching together to Victory!

I have full confidence in your courage, devotion to duty and skill in battle. We will accept nothing less than full Victory!

Good Luck! And let us all beseech the blessing of Almighty God·upon this great and noble undertaking.

Dwight Eisenhower

"In case of failure", is a draft of a little-known message written by General Dwight D. Eisenhower just before the D-Day invasion in the event that the landings failed.

Ike had composed another text, less glorious, to be released in case the landings failed. Fortunately, he never needed to read this document. It was found by his aide, weeks after D- Day. In this text, by fully assuming his responsibilities and recognising his mistakes, Eisenhower pays tribute to the courage of the men he had sent into combat. It read:

"*Our landings have failed and I have withdrawn the troops. My decision to attack at this time and place was based upon the best information available. The troops, the air and the Navy did all that bravery and devotion to duty could do. If any blame or fault attaches to the attempt it is mine alone.*"

THE PRAYER OF LIEUTENANT COLONEL WOLVERTON

CHAPTER 2

On the evening of June 5, perched on a mound overlooking his men who stood gathered in front of him and imploring the protection of Almighty God, Lieutenant Colonel Wolverton read his personal prayer out loud, conveying to his men what the death of man really meant.

It took them all by surprise as he addressed them with this sincere and moving narrative: "*Men, I am not a religious man and I don't know your feelings in this matter, but I am going to ask you to pray with me for the success of the mission before us. And while we pray, let us get on our knees and not look down but up with faces raised to the sky.*"

One soldier, still moved by what he had heard, remembered that Wolverton spoke to them simply, just as if he were one of them. He seemed genuinely concerned by the prospect that they would not all come back alive. No one spoke during this time, and you could hear a pin drop.

Wolverton then read the prayer he had composed for the occasion:

> *God almighty!*
> *In a few short hours we will be in battle with the enemy.*
> *We do not join battle afraid.*
> *We do not ask favours or indulgence but ask that, if You will, use us as Your instrument for the right and an aid in returning peace to the world.*
> *We do not know or seek what our fate will be. We ask only this, that if die we must, that we die as men would die, without complaining, without pleading and safe in the feeling that we have done our best for what we believed was right.*
> *Oh Lord, protect our loved ones and be near us in the fire ahead and with us now as we pray to you.*

The last words still resonated in the heads of Wolverton's men as they stood up. He also make an appointment with them at Kansas City, one year after the war, to celebrate the first anniversary of D-Day, because he did not doubt for a moment that the operation in which the 3rd/506th PIR was now going to be plunged would hasten the fall of the Third Reich.

This meeting did indeed take place, but with a year's delay, on June 6, 1946. Unfortunately without the one who had the original idea. Many soldiers of the 3rd Battalion also missed the call. Four men from Lieutenant Bobuck's group never saw the United States again.

A few days before landing, Wolverton shared with his officers the presentiment that he may not survive the war. He wrote twenty-one letters to his son Lachlan, who was still only an infant. A letter was to be delivered to him on each birthday until he reached twenty-one. The letters were only to be opened in the event of his death. Ed Shames recalls with emotion the privileged moments he shared with Wolverton in trying to find the right words while putting these letters together. Ray Calandrella also helped with this epistolary work.

" We will always remember the paratroopers who landed in St. Come on June 6, 1944, these fearless and spirited young men who so courageously attacked an enemy so embedded and so strong. What a training these men must have had to have made them what they are! "

Gustave Laurence, Mayor of Saint-Côme-du-Mont in 1944 (from letter dated 16 June 1945) .

History and organization

The 506th PIR was created in the United States Army on July 1, 1942. Activated at Camp Toccoa, Georgia on July 20, 1942, it was moved to Fort Benning in December of the same year. It was attached to the 101st Airborne Division in June 1943.

The 3rd Battalion was composed of three companies (codenamed G, H, I: George, How, Item) and a command company (HQ/3rd/506th PIR). Robert Lee Wolverton was in command until his death on June 6, 1944.

Shoulder patch of the 101st Airborne Division, the "Screaming Eagles".

Unlike the shoulder insignia of the 101st Airborne Division, the following badges were not worn on battle dress. The ParaDice Patch was usually placed to the left side, on the breast pocket on sports clothing or officers leather jackets.

Oval tricolour found on the serviceman's shirt, also on the left side of the chest.

The Regimental Crest enamel was worn on the service jacket.

HQ/3rd/506th PIR, Fort Bragg, July 1943.
Standing in the first row, left to right:
1st man - Jack W Harrison; 5th man - Sergeant William Pauli; 7th man - Chief Sergeant Ed Shames; 12th man - Lieutenant Colonel Robert Lee Wolverton; 17th man - John Anthony Taormina.
2nd row, left to right: 13th man - Raymond E. Calandrella.
Back row, left to right: 10th man - Joseph F. Gorenc; 11th man - Donald Clifton Ross; 18th man - John A. Rinehart.

From left to right: Pauli, Harrison, Bradley.

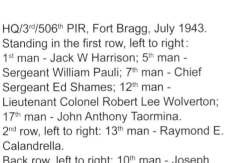

D-Day Mission

The disembarkation of the US 7th Corps in the Utah Beach area, as early as possible, to capture the deep-water port of Cherbourg - a primary objective.

General Bradley, fully aware that the C-47s, carrying paratroopers and flying at low altitude, would prompt heavy fire from the ground as they crossed the French coast, assumed the risk of heavy losses. On June 6, 1944, Wolverton's men were parachuted behind Utah Beach, which was held by enemy troops. They needed to take control of two bridges crossing the river Douve, two kilometres east of Carentan, and prevent by all possible means German reinforcements getting through to Utah beach.

A section of the 326th Airborne Engineer Battalion and two demolition crews were attached to the 3rd/506th PIR. They would get ready for the destruction of the bridges in case this became necessary.

Allied aerial reconnaissance photograph of the River Douve near the village of Brévands, dated 24 December 1943. The highway bridge situated left is under construction, one of the objectives tasked to the 3rd/506th PIR.

Charles Everett Bullard, Crew Chief of one of the C-47s used to train Krebs, later pronounced that "*These troops would subsequently participate in the mission assigned to the 101st Airborne, who needed to capture and hold the strategic town of Carentan, to secure and maintain for our troops the roads and bridges, preventing enemy reinforcement. The U.S. 4th Infantry Division, arriving by sea, would join the attack.*"

The 506th PIR would return with the 101st Airborne to England in July, mission accomplished, but with heavy losses.

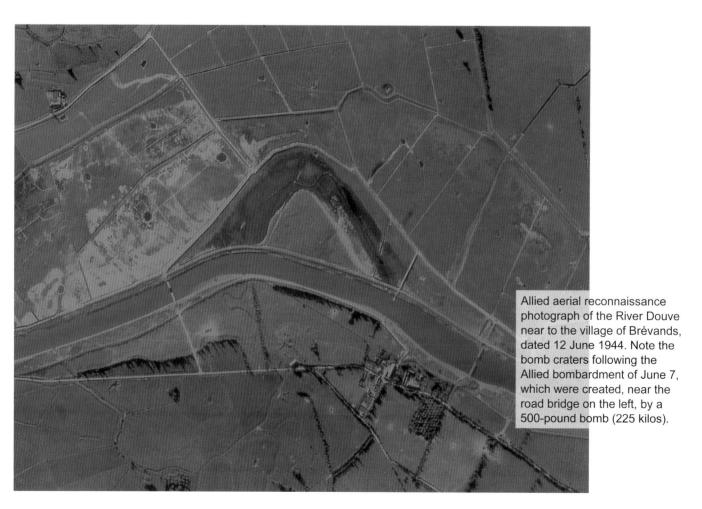

Allied aerial reconnaissance photograph of the River Douve near to the village of Brévands, dated 12 June 1944. Note the bomb craters following the Allied bombardment of June 7, which were created, near the road bridge on the left, by a 500-pound bomb (225 kilos).

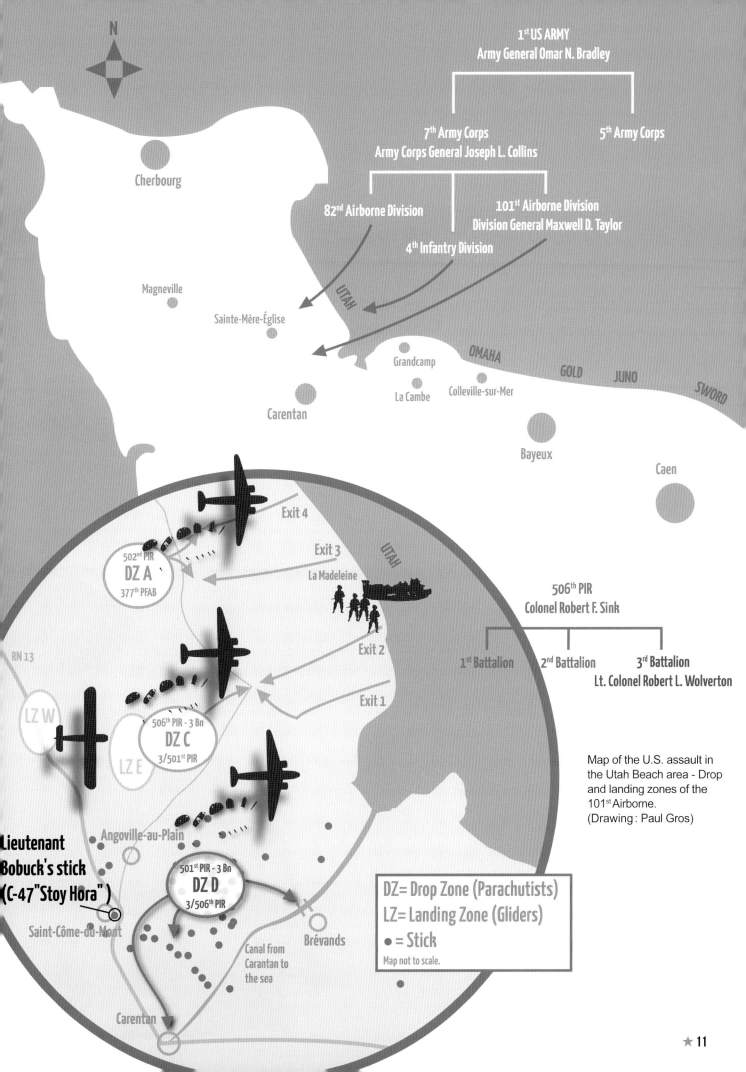

1st US ARMY
Army General Omar N. Bradley

7th Army Corps
Army Corps General Joseph L. Collins

5th Army Corps

82nd Airborne Division

4th Infantry Division

101st Airborne Division
Division General Maxwell D. Taylor

Cherbourg

Magneville

Sainte-Mère-Église

UTAH

Grandcamp

OMAHA

GOLD

JUNO

SWORD

La Cambe

Colleville-sur-Mer

Carentan

Bayeux

Caen

Exit 4

Exit 3

502nd PIR
DZ A
377th PFAB

La Madeleine

UTAH

506th PIR
Colonel Robert F. Sink

RN 13

Exit 2

Exit 1

1st Battalion

2nd Battalion

3rd Battalion
Lt. Colonel Robert L. Wolverton

LZ W

506th PIR - 3 Bn
DZ C
3/501st PIR

LZ E

Map of the U.S. assault in
the Utah Beach area - Drop
and landing zones of the
101st Airborne.
(Drawing : Paul Gros)

Lieutenant
Bobuck's stick
(C-47 "Stoy Hora")

Angoville-au-Plain

501st PIR - 3 Bn
DZ D
3/506th PIR

Saint-Côme-du-Mont

Brévands

DZ= Drop Zone (Parachutists)
LZ= Landing Zone (Gliders)
• = Stick
Map not to scale.

Canal from
Carentan to
the sea

Carentan

★ 11

One by one, the sixteen paratroopers of Bobuck's stick boarded the "Stoy Hora". Some were so heavily laden with weapons and equipment that they needed to be hoisted into the aircraft.

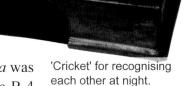

Attention should be drawn to two men amongst the paratroopers who took their places in the hold of the *Stoy Hora* that night. Their faces were not blackened, their uniforms were different and they were not holding a weapon in hand. On board Sergeant John Nagy, Crew Chief of the *Stoy Hora* was wearing two parachutes - a main and a reserve, a B-4 lifejacket - nicknamed the Mae West, a steel helmet without camouflage safety net, a 45 calibre revolver attached to the belt and a protective flak jacket. This vest was the only protection he had against the German Flak (anti-aircraft guns).

While boarding the *Stoy Hora*, Nagy gave the BBC reporter, Ward Smith, the same equipment he himself was wearing, with the exception of the revolver. Smith is the only character in this book whose face we have no knowledge of, he has left no known photographs. In the illustrations, we have chosen to clad him in an English paratrooper's jacket, the famous Denison Smock, as worn by his BBC Australian counterpart "Chester Wilmot" who was covering the disembarkment in the English sector, more to the east. But Smith, the man without a face, has left the sound of his voice on a recording made in June 1944, entitled *Flight With American Airborne*.

The paratroopers had donned the reinforced 1942 model jump-kit composed of jacket and trousers held up by braces, over their regulatory underclothes of woollen vest and leggings The shoulder patch of the 101st Airborne was sewn onto the top of the left sleeve. The men of this unit were not wearing the American flag on their right sleeve.

Around their necks hung the legendary **cricket**, as well as **dog tags** – the engraved nameplates displaying the name and surname of the para, service number, blood type, religion and name and address of person to be notified in case of death. The paratroopers of HQ/3rd/506th

Dog Tags.

'Cricket' for recognising each other at night.

PIR also had a white silk scarf tied around their necks, on which was printed a map of France, an indispensable accessory to orientate themselves in this unknown land occupied by the enemy.

Over their woollen socks, they were proudly wearing the characteristic jump boots that differentiated them from the other soldiers of the airborne infantry, who were transported in gliders (towed aircraft without engines). Dressed as simple infantrymen, the gliders were unjustly treated by their paratrooper counterparts who felt themselves to be superior. A single visit to the interior of a Waco glider is enough to appreciate the boldness and courage of these men, who went to fight in such

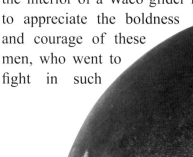

Bill Atlee's M1C Helmet.

vehicles, composed of a light wooden and metal structure and covered with coated canvas.

All the men displayed an ace of spades on each side of their **M1C helmet**, which identified the 506th PIR. The 3rd battalion normally had a white dot to the left of the ace of spades. However, one has observed some helmets where the white dot is to the right of the ace of spades. The officers' helmet had a white vertical stripe to the rear, while the sub-officers' had a horizontal stripe. These stripes permitted men to identify their chiefs in the heat of the action.

John Rinehart and Charles Riley carried a **U.S. carbine M1 A1** whose handle was curved, inside a special cover. William Atlee and Alex Bobuck carried with them a **M3 Grease Gun submachine gun**. William Pauli had taken apart and stored his **Garand rifle** in a **Griswold Bag** transport jacket that he had slid under his parachute. This special jacket was designed to protect the paratrooper and his weapon during the jump. Sergeant Ed Shames rendered his Garand ready to deploy, pressed under the strap of the parachute harness in order to use his gun as soon as he touched the ground. Ed had never encountered any problems during the many jumps he had made and Harry Howard and Ray Calandrella were the same. John Taormina, Joe Gorenc, Jack Harrison, Donald Ross, Anthony Wincenciak and Jesse Cross were heavily armed with bulky **Thompson submachine guns**.

Harrison, from the transmissions section of HQ/3rd/506th PIR, was carrying an **M-209**, a manual machine to encode and decode messages transmitted between two units. In order to keep it secret, each operator was ordered to destroy the machine if it risked falling into enemy hands.

M3 Grease Gun submachine gun.

Ed Shames is probably the only man from the 3rd/506th PIR who did not have time to blacken his face on June 5, as he had received the order by Lieutenant Colonel Wolverton to stay in the map tent until the last minute. The other soldiers would probably clean up their faces throughout the day on the 6, as soon as they were able.

U.S. M1 A1 Carbine.

Thompson submachine gun.

Harrison (right) is holding a Thompson submachine gun. On his left side, note the small pouch containing the cipher machine. Pauli has slid the Griswold bag under his reserve parachute.

Garand rifle and Griswold Bag.

Cipher Machine.

Message Book M-210-A
Signal Corps, U. S. Army

MESSAGE BOOK
M-210-B
Signal Corps, U. S. Army

Rope supplied to paratroopers for the jump. It often proved beneficial for getting out of a bad situation, whether it be descending a tree or sliding along a church roof.

D-Day, Gustave Laurence, the Mayor of Saint-Côme-du-Mont and roofer by trade, was climbing a ladder at the request of the German soldiers in order to unhook an American paratrooper who was still on the roof of the house opposite the church, his feet were caught in electrical wiring and his back was leaning against the roof of the house. In a letter dated June 16, 1945, he noted with these few telling words: "*A paratrooper in full equipment is very heavy.*" Indeed, for the grand jump, some of the men, once fully equipped and armed, weighed twice their own weight! Charles Everett Bullard testifies to this: "*It was really surprising to see all these big and robust soldiers coming towards the plane with all their equipment attached to them, needing to be hoisted on board by a ladder. Just imagine a normal sized man weighing about 70 kilos with equipment weighing about 55 kilos tied to him*."

In addition to the equipment visible on the paratrooper, inside his pockets and his knapsack our man was also carrying French invasion vouchers, cigarettes, tobacco, a pipe, a spoon. An M2 penknife switchblade was housed in a small vertical pocket on the left under the collar of the jump jacket, servicing the paratrooper for a quick release from the parachute lines if he became tangled up during the landing.

T-5 dorsal (primary) parachute

Note the long cover jacket for the U.S. M1 A1 rifle, between the 1942 first aid kit attached to the belt and the pair of leather gloves.

Silk scarf on which was printed a map of the invasion.

The invasion map was also carried in special pouches.

T-5 ventral (reserve) parachute.

Container with pigeons responsible for transmitting secret messages.

Hawkins antitank mine.

Gammon grenade Type 82.

Angled lamp.

Bands of brown and green fabrics.

MKII Fragmentation grenade

Individual paratrooper dressing kit.

FIRST - AID

Paratroopers' helmets were covered with a camouflage net of medium brown mesh. In the archival photos of June 4, only Anthony Wincenciak is topped with **strips of brown and green canvas**.

The **individual dressing kit** was carried with the equipment or on the body, but not on the helmet as shown by mistake in the film *The Longest Day*. This historic detail has been confirmed by veterans and specialist historians.

M1936 suspension braces.

Gas detection arm band.

FIRST AID

M1 Relief cartridge pouch.

M1918 Cartridge pouch belt.

M1 Garand rifle equipped with bayonet.

M3 combat knife with sheath.

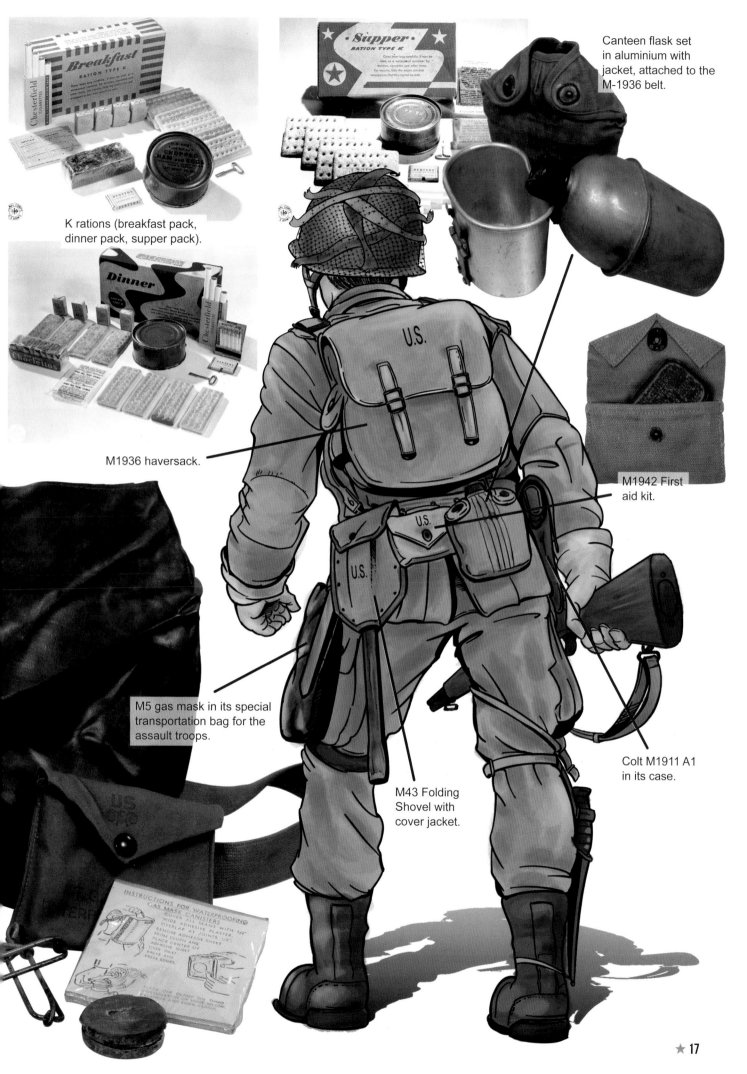

K rations (breakfast pack, dinner pack, supper pack).

M1936 haversack.

M5 gas mask in its special transportation bag for the assault troops.

M43 Folding Shovel with cover jacket.

Canteen flask set in aluminium with jacket, attached to the M-1936 belt.

M1942 First aid kit.

Colt M1911 A1 in its case.

Wolverton was carrying hardware specific to officers: **card holder**, **binoculars**, a compass. Original detail: he had hanging under his belt a Marine Corps reversible camouflage poncho.

Garrison cap sporting a distinctive round badge for the airborne units. From April 1942, it was placed on the left for enlisted men and NCOs, and on the right for officers.

Binoculars.

M38 Card holder and its contents.

Mae West: lifejacket, distributed to all American paratroopers who flew over the English Channel. The letters "RS" indicate the initials of the head of the 506th PIR, Colonel Robert Sink. This vest therefore belonged to a paratrooper from this regiment.

M1911 A1 Colt and its case.

Red Cross Armbands.

1944 Kit model for officer with instruments for minor surgery.

Designed to be laced inside the type II nursing bag, the insert would hold 6 hard rubber tubes used to keep pills and capsules. The contents of this satchel was different for the officer and the nurse. It was worn over the shoulder with a strap on the opposite shoulder. Nurse Newell's nursing bag contained scissors for dressings and bandages, necessary items for care of burns, triangular swabs, iodine solution washes, ammonia salts, individual dressings and bandages. Doctor Morgan's satchel was more complete and included safety pins, a thermometer, syringes of morphine, a Hypodermic Set (metal box with syringes for subcutaneous application), boxes and sachets of sulfanilamide (antibiotics).

Captain Morgan Stanley, Surgeon with the 3rd/506th PIR and Sergeant Nurse Thomas Newell would carry equipment specific to medical personnel. The Geneva Convention prohibited them from carrying arms. They relied on good fortune, their sense of responsibility and the international Red Cross armband as their only means of protection. On D-Day, Morgan was wearing the armband on his left arm, Newell had one on each arm.

Although the medical staff could wear belt model 1936 equipped with special suspension braces, on which hung two nursing type II satchels, the two medics from Bobuck's stick were only wearing one shoulder satchel for the Normandy drop.

(All medical equipment is derived from the book *The way we were No. 3, Mc DOC Ilvoy and his parachuting medics*, where they are presented in detail)

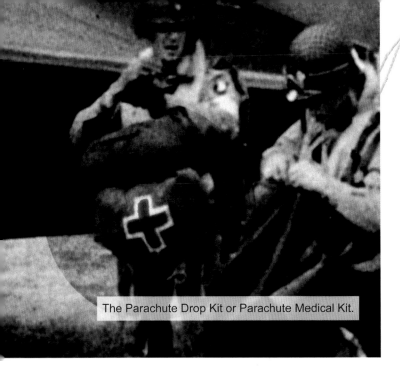

The Parachute Drop Kit or Parachute Medical Kit.

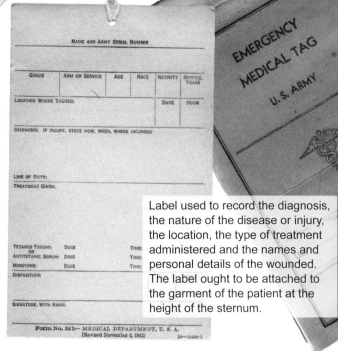

NAME AND ARMY SERIAL NUMBER

| GRADE | ARM OR SERVICE | AGE | RACE | NATIVITY | SERVICE YEARS |

LOCATION WHERE TAGGED: DATE   HOUR

DIAGNOSIS: IF INJURY, STATE HOW, WHEN, WHERE INCURRED

LINE OF DUTY:
TREATMENT GIVEN:

TETANUS TOXOID: DOSE   TIME:
OR
ANTITETANIC SERUM: DOSE   TIME:
MORPHINE: DOSE   TIME:
DISPOSITION:

SIGNATURE, WITH RANK:

Form No. 52b— MEDICAL DEPARTMENT, U. S. A.
(Revised November 6, 1942)   16—15434-1

EMERGENCY MEDICAL TAG U. S. ARMY

Label used to record the diagnosis, the nature of the disease or injury, the location, the type of treatment administered and the names and personal details of the wounded. The label ought to be attached to the garment of the patient at the height of the sternum.

The history of Captain E. Morgan's flight jacket testified that Franco-American friendship endures and is transmitted from generation to generation. In March 2006 this jacket was offered to Philippe Esvelin by the daughter of the veteran Bernard J. Ryan, a Doctor with the 506th/PIR, in whom Morgan had confided before his death.

Philippe Esvelin , the author of *D -Day Gliders* published by Heimdal in 2001, had made several trips to the United States. During his research on the use of gliders that had transported the men of the 82nd and 101st Airborne Division in Normandy, he met Robert C. Casey, glider pilot with the 436th TCG detached to the 437th transporting the 82nd Airborne Division. Robert had introduced Bernard J. Ryan to him. Shortly after the death of her father Bernard, his daughter Kathleen sent a parcel from America on February 13, 2005 to Philippe Esvelin. Imagine Philippe's emotion and astonishment when he discovered the precious contents of the package: the jacket that had belonged to Captain Stanley E. Morgan, service number 0-417912.

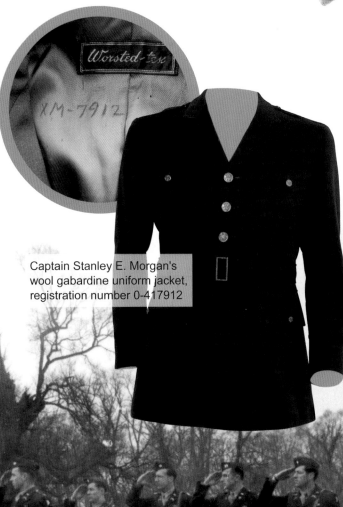

Captain Stanley E. Morgan's wool gabardine uniform jacket, registration number 0-417912

Littlecote, England, March 18, 1944. Captain Morgan is the second man on the right.

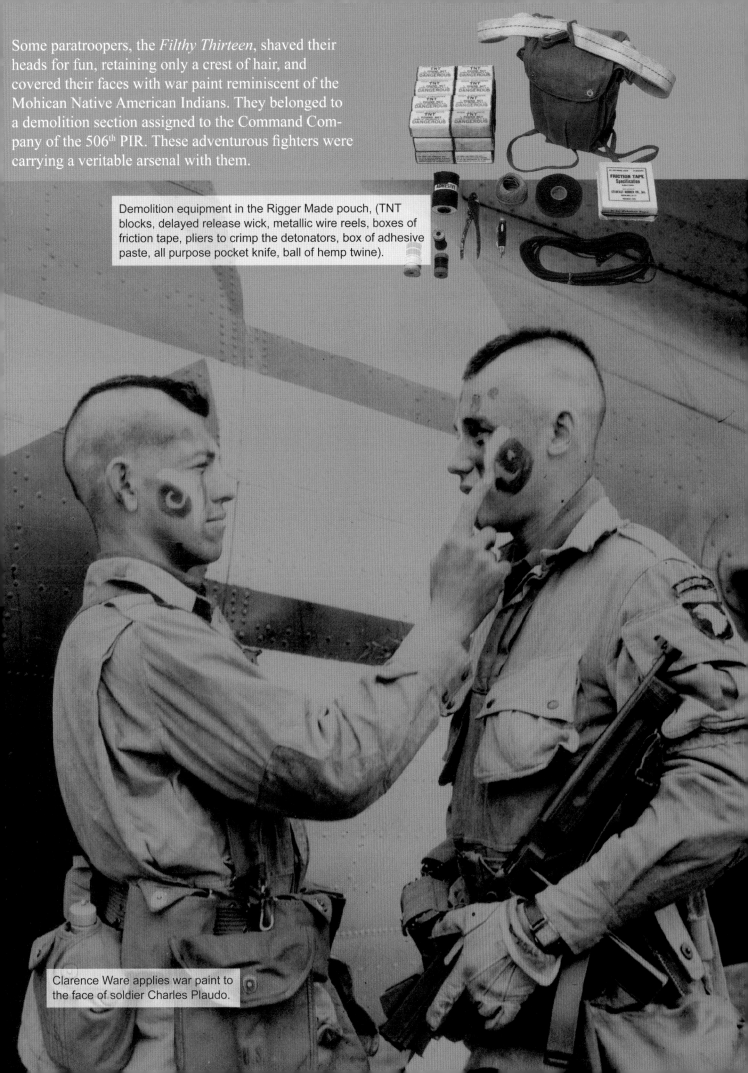

Some paratroopers, the *Filthy Thirteen*, shaved their heads for fun, retaining only a crest of hair, and covered their faces with war paint reminiscent of the Mohican Native American Indians. They belonged to a demolition section assigned to the Command Company of the 506th PIR. These adventurous fighters were carrying a veritable arsenal with them.

Demolition equipment in the Rigger Made pouch, (TNT blocks, delayed release wick, metallic wire reels, boxes of friction tape, pliers to crimp the detonators, box of adhesive paste, all purpose pocket knife, ball of hemp twine).

Clarence Ware applies war paint to the face of soldier Charles Plaudo.

With the landings in view, Lieutenant Colonel Wolverton's men had been subjected to two years of very hard training necessary for airborne troops. They had still not seen active combat. Normandy would be their baptism of fire...

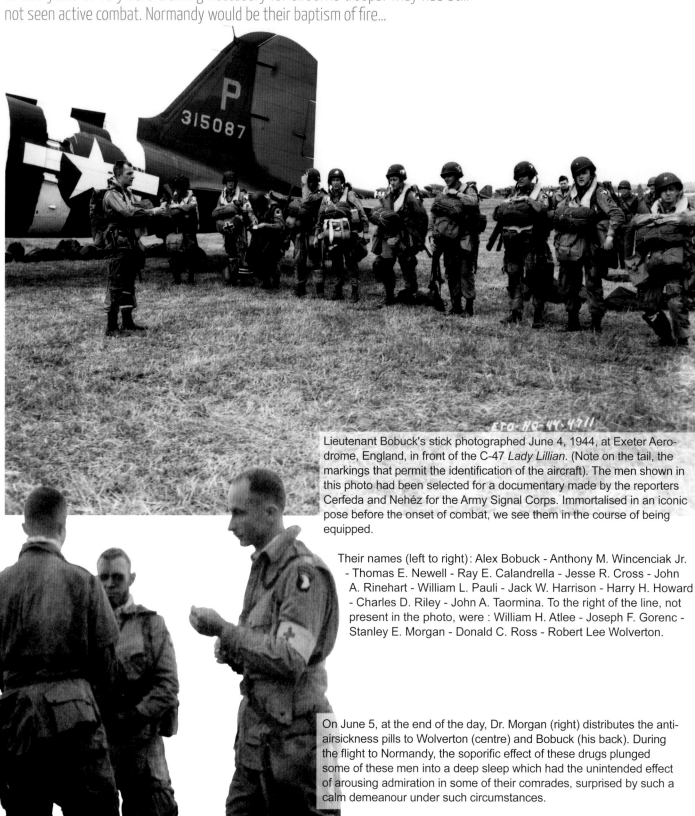

Lieutenant Bobuck's stick photographed June 4, 1944, at Exeter Aerodrome, England, in front of the C-47 *Lady Lillian*. (Note on the tail, the markings that permit the identification of the aircraft). The men shown in this photo had been selected for a documentary made by the reporters Cerfeda and Nehéz for the Army Signal Corps. Immortalised in an iconic pose before the onset of combat, we see them in the course of being equipped.

Their names (left to right): Alex Bobuck - Anthony M. Wincenciak Jr. - Thomas E. Newell - Ray E. Calandrella - Jesse R. Cross - John A. Rinehart - William L. Pauli - Jack W. Harrison - Harry H. Howard - Charles D. Riley - John A. Taormina. To the right of the line, not present in the photo, were : William H. Atlee - Joseph F. Gorenc - Stanley E. Morgan - Donald C. Ross - Robert Lee Wolverton.

On June 5, at the end of the day, Dr. Morgan (right) distributes the anti-airsickness pills to Wolverton (centre) and Bobuck (his back). During the flight to Normandy, the soporific effect of these drugs plunged some of these men into a deep sleep which had the unintended effect of arousing admiration in some of their comrades, surprised by such a calm demeanour under such circumstances.

Bobuck helps Gorenc to put on his main dorsal parachute.

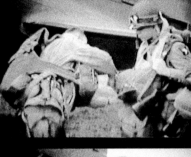

Bobuck and Calandrella (note on Calandrella's helmet, the Polaroid M-1944 protective goggles and the non-regulation gun at Bobuck's side).

Wincenciak is assisted by a GI wearing an infantry uniform. Note the aluminium pocket sized canteen set slid into the little pocket of his work pants.

Bobuck and Cross.

Rinehart, the *pigeon man*, and Cross kneeling.

Ross, last man under Bobuck, takes his turn to board the C -47.

Bobuck (right) inspects Howard's main dorsal parachute (left). In the queue, Riley, Taormina, and Atlee await their turn.

Photo taken inside the C-47 *Lady Lilian*, on June 4. The men who have not blackened their faces look relaxed and smiling.

From back to front left: Wincenciak (helmet covered in camouflage strips), Cross, Pauli, Howard, Riley, Gorenc (cigarette in hand), Ross (of whom we can only see the left knee).

From back to front right: Nurse Newell (bareheaded) Calandrella (with the goggles on the helmet), Rinehart (John with his head drawn back, the pigeon containers placed on his knee enable his identification), Harrison, Taormina, Atlee (cigarette in mouth), Morgan (lighting a cigarette).

ETO-HQ-44-4705

377578

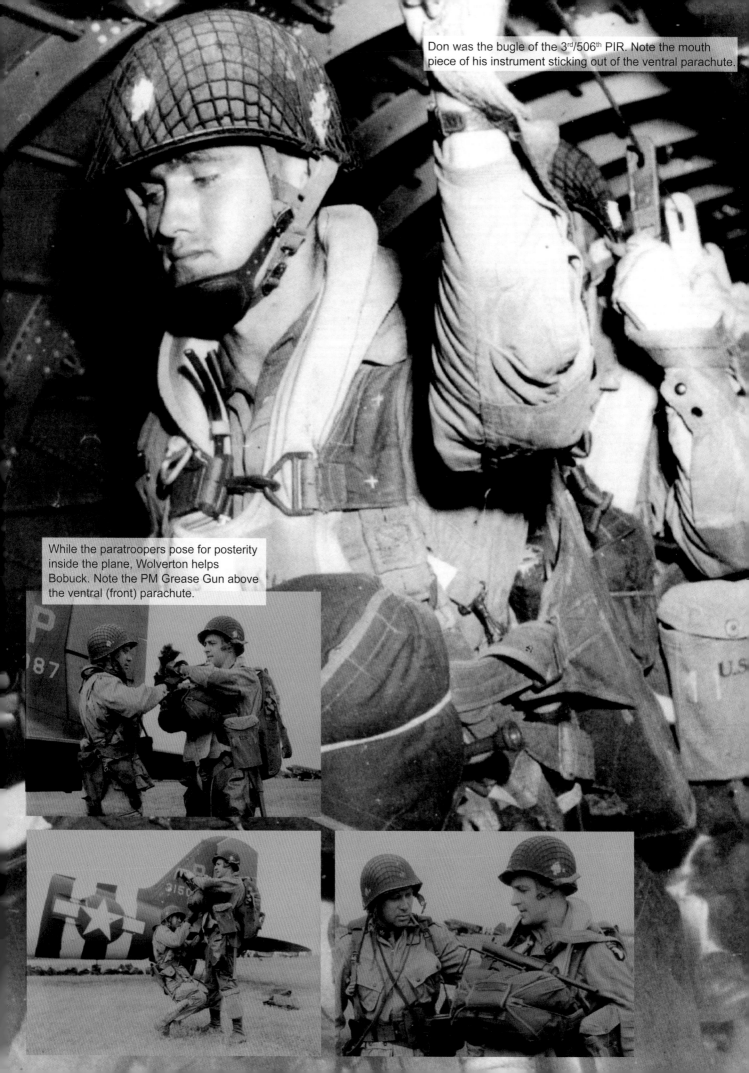

Don was the bugle of the 3rd/506th PIR. Note the mouth piece of his instrument sticking out of the ventral parachute.

While the paratroopers pose for posterity inside the plane, Wolverton helps Bobuck. Note the PM Grease Gun above the ventral (front) parachute.

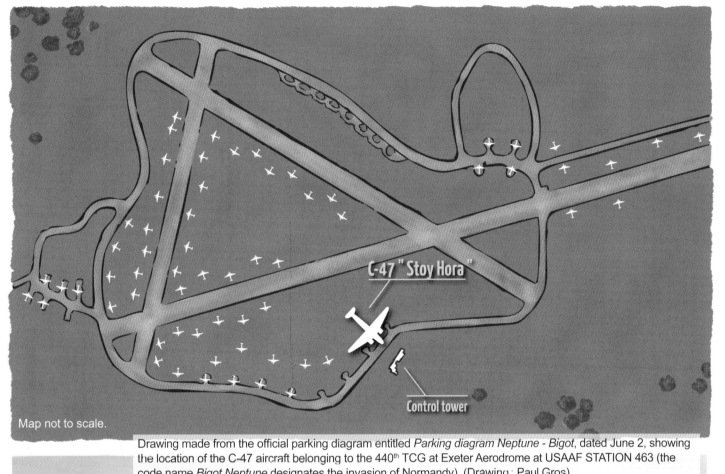

C-47 "Stoy Hora"

Control tower

Map not to scale.

Drawing made from the official parking diagram entitled *Parking diagram Neptune - Bigot*, dated June 2, showing the location of the C-47 aircraft belonging to the 440th TCG at Exeter Aerodrome at USAAF STATION 463 (the code name *Bigot Neptune* designates the invasion of Normandy). (Drawing: Paul Gros)

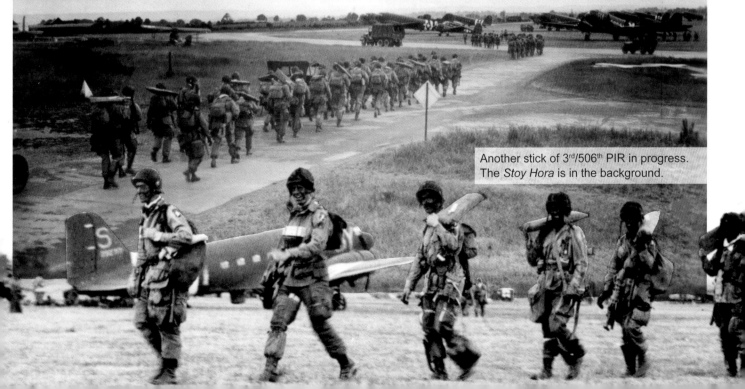

The PIR 3rd/506th en route towards the aircraft on June 5, 1944. The C-47 to the right of the image is the *Stoy Hora*.

Another stick of 3rd/506th PIR in progress. The *Stoy Hora* is in the background.

A group of Wolverton's team in front of the *Stoy Hora*. Note to the right of the door, the hatched "1" drawn in chalk to identify the command aircraft piloted by Krebs. The door is still in place, it will be removed before takeoff. Veterans of the Troop Carrier Group and of the 101st Airborne Division have testified unanimously that the C-47 flew without doors on an airdrop mission. The paratroopers have blackened their faces. From left to right: two unidentified men, Morgan (note the medical armband on his left arm) Bobuck (note the extra pockets sewn on the bottom of the jump jacket), Cross, Bob Wolverton, Bill Atlee (whose head is higher than that of the other men), Howard, Don Ross, Tom Newell (note the medical armband on his left arm), Joe Gorenc.

Relaxing before takeoff. Ross smiles broadly. Atlee, relaxed, is lying on the floor.

Joe Gorenc hoists himself on board the *Stoy Hora* to join his comrades.

Shortly before takeoff, Wolverton, looking wistful (centre) is flanked by the smiling Lieutenant Colonel Krebs (right) and Major Howard Cannon (left). Note the Flak Vest worn by Cannon and the headbands worn by both pilots.
Less than three hours after this photo, Wolverton will be dead.

Krebs, who has just donned his Flak Vest, takes his turn to board the C-47. The paratrooper already seated near the door is Donald Ross. He will be the second man to jump, immediately after Wolverton.

Robert Lee Wolverton equips himself. Note on his back, the poncho hung on the belt.

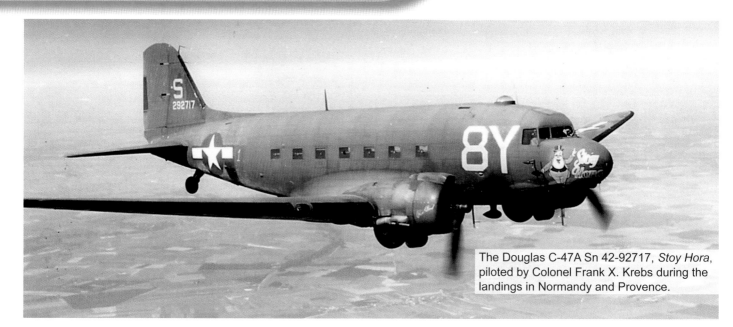

The Douglas C-47A Sn 42-92717, *Stoy Hora*, piloted by Colonel Frank X. Krebs during the landings in Normandy and Provence.

The Douglas DC-3 is a remarkable aircraft that has proved reliable during the course of its air service, even in the face of great difficulty, enabling the industrial development of modern air transport since its first civilian flight in the United States in December 1935. Unsightly on the ground, it was pure grace in flight and as Randy Hils has emphasised, the pilots adored it. The first models of the 10,000 DC-3s built for the army emerged from the factories shortly before the entry of the United States into World War II.

Designated as the C-47 *Skytrain* by the American Air Force, after having received a few minor modifications, it began its military career as a transporter of merchandise. But the development of airborne troops, from 1942, quickly necessitated an exceptional aircraft that was rapid, powerful, robust, fitted with seats to transport paratroopers and equipped with wide doors for easy loading. Thus the C-47 (also known as the *Dakota*, the English name, and *Gooney Bird*), was the natural choice for transporting troops and making drops.

Historian Randy Hils states elsewhere that it was decided at the outset, in the world of troop transportation, that there should not under any circumstances be the addition of shielding to the C-47 for protection of paratroopers and crew, which would have sacrificed its payload capacity. In this respect the aircraft would also not be equipped with self-sealing fuel tanks even in cases were they might be penetrated by projectiles and it would not be furnished with any weapons, three essential characteristics that held true for other military aircraft.

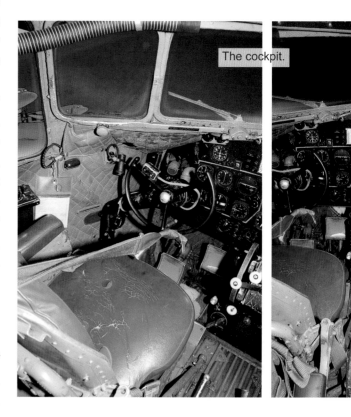

The cockpit.

Delivered on February 16, 1944, for D-Day, the *Stoy Hora* joined the 98th Squadron of the 440th TCG of the 9th Air Force. Following this it was designated to the 1st Squadron scouts in December 1944, then to the 97th TCS in May 1945, it was transferred on July 11 1946, from Hanau (Germany) to Prague-Ruzyne Airport. After the war, on March 6, 1947, it was then passed to the OK-WDK in Czechoslovakia.

The *Stoy Hora*, which had managed to escape particularly deadly anti-aircraft fire over Normandy, met a tragic end ten years after D-Day. On December 12, 1954, during a simple goods transportation, it crashed at Pezinok, about fifteen kilometres from the runway at Bratislava - Ivanka, Czechoslovakia with its crew, who were killed instantly.

The crew

D-Day, the *Stoy Hora* was transporting sixteen paratroopers from Lieutenant Bobuck's group, including the Commanding Officer of the 3rd/506th PIR, Lieutenant-Colonel Robert Lee Wolverton. Ward Smith, the British war correspondent working for the BBC, had joined the group at the last minute. The C-47 was piloted by Lieutenant-Colonel Frank X. Krebs, assisted by Major Howard W. Cannon (co-pilot). Two navigators, Lieutenant Edward Sullivan and Sub-Lieutenant George T. Arnold as well as Staff Sergeant Bill Quick

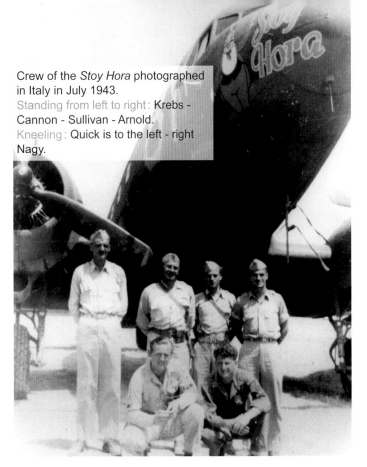

Crew of the *Stoy Hora* photographed in Italy in July 1943.
Standing from left to right: Krebs - Cannon - Sullivan - Arnold.
Kneeling: Quick is to the left - right Nagy.

 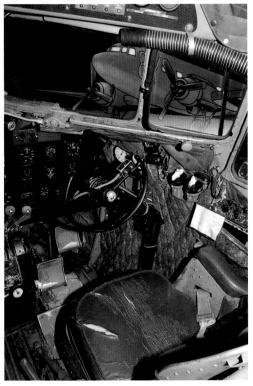

Factory of Manufacture: Oklahoma City, Oklahoma
Contract number: AC- 28405
Cn. 12549 C- 47A -10- DK Sn. 42-92717
Engines: 2 engines: Pratt & Whitney R-1830-92 Twin Wasp radial piston 1200 Horsepower
Weight when empty: 7 750 kg
Max. load: 12 701 kg
Wingspan: 28.95 m
Length: 19.66 m
Height: 5.17 m
Max. speed: 350 à 370 km / h
Cruising speed: 270 km / h
Service Ceiling: 7 000 to 7,350 m
Range: 3825 Km
Radius of action: 2175 km
No Arms
Number built: 13,177 (all builders)
Number of units still operational (all versions): 300-400
Average hourly consumption: 140 to 150 U.S. gallons AV -GAS 91 Octane (530-560 litres)
2.5 litres of lubricant
Usual crew: 4-5 men
Passenger transport: 16-18 paratroopers equipped for combat or 4536 kg of cargo

Features and technical specifications of the *Stoy Hora* extracted from the C-47 Flight Manual published by the U.S. Army Air Force.

(radio-operator) and Sergeant John Nagy (Crew-Chief) completed the crew. Charles Everett Bullard says that *"Nagy was a hell of a Crew-Chief"*, this goes without saying since he was flying with Krebs, who always required the maximum from his men.

In this drawing, note that the red ambient light corresponds to the lighting authorised at the beginning of the flight, while the *Stoy Hora* was still flying over England. As soon as it leaves the friendly zone all interior and exterior lights are extinguished, plunging the men into darkness. Only nine small blue lights invisible from the ground remain, located on top of the aircraft.

Five crew members take their place at the front of the plane. The pilot to the left, the co-pilot to the right. Behind them in the alcoves of the cabin leading to the hold, sits the radio-operator and a navigator. We have simplified the cabin in the interests easy use. Bullard recalls that the radio operator sat behind the pilot and co-pilot. He adds that the navigator used the same table as the radio-operator as well as the Astrodome. There were two navigators on the C-47 at the head of the formation, note the second who is looking through the glass bubble. Thus, all crew members, were at the front of the plane, with the exception of the sixth man, the Crew-Chief, who always sat near the door during combat missions.

In the drawing, John Nagy stands at the rear of the hold and gives instructions to the paratroopers who are sitting face to face on the seats running along the walls of the C-47. Colonel Wolverton took his place next to the door because he will jump first. To his right sits Bobuck, the leader of the stick who will leave the plane in the last position to ensure that all the men have left the C-47.

The reporter Ward Smith will not jump with the paratroopers. Sitting on the first seat to the left of the communication door leading to the cockpit, he will return to England where he must complete his article.

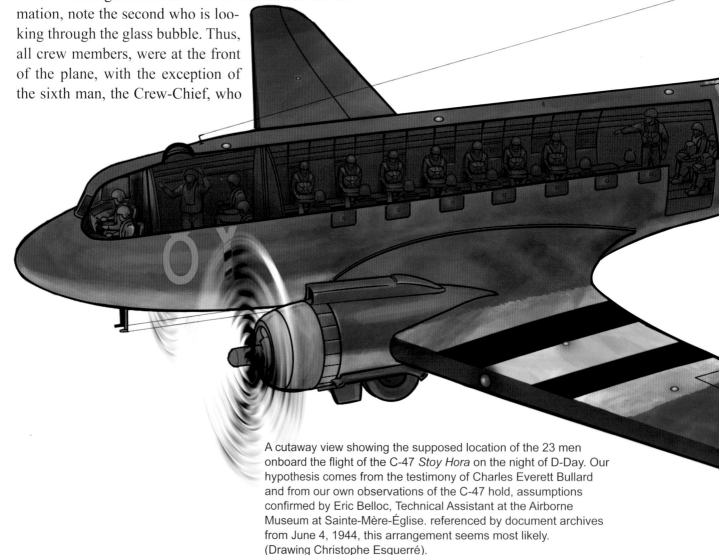

A cutaway view showing the supposed location of the 23 men onboard the flight of the C-47 *Stoy Hora* on the night of D-Day. Our hypothesis comes from the testimony of Charles Everett Bullard and from our own observations of the C-47 hold, assumptions confirmed by Eric Belloc, Technical Assistant at the Airborne Museum at Sainte-Mère-Église. referenced by document archives from June 4, 1944, this arrangement seems most likely. (Drawing Christophe Esquerré).

Briefing by Frank X. Krebs.

Note the paint applied in a hurry to the C-47 *Lady Lillian*, before which stands Lieutenant Bobuck.

During the troop transportation missions, the aircraft flew with the door open in order to facilitate the exit of the paratroopers, although Ward Smith seems to indicate in his report that the door of the *Stoy Hora* had been closed after takeoff and then opened at the moment of jumping.

Each plane displayed an original drawing on its nose, hand painted and non-regulatory, known by the term "Nose Art". The mystery of the *Stoy Hora* is revealed to us in an Appendix. Charles Everett Bullard sheds some more light on the C-47 markings: "*In the final hours before disembarkment, to prevent the allied fleet and the anti-aircraft batteries coastal defence firing on friendly aircraft by error, wide alternately arranged black and white lines were painted around the fuselage and on the wings of each aircraft.*"

The lack of identification had cost the Allies dear in July 1943 during the airborne assault in Sicily. On 11 July, 23 aircraft were shot down by the anti-aircraft artillery from the allied fleet, and they deplored the loss of the 81 killed and 148 wounded and missing from the ranks of the 504th PIR of the 82nd Airborne. ★ 31

THE 440th TROOP CARRIER GROUP

The 440th Troop Carrier Group was formed on May 25, 1943 and put into service on 1 July 1943 at Baer Field, Indiana. Two other bases in the United States would temporarily welcome it during the initial period : the main training centre for troops of the airborne Alliance, at Nebraska, and at Pope Field, Fort Bragg, in North Carolina.

D uring the year 1943, the pilots of the 440th TCG were trained tirelessly in the finer techniques of the parachute drop, of re-supplying and of towing gliders which during low altitude flights are especially perilous. As explained Randy Hils : "*During the long flights across the country, the pilots had perfected their competence for night operations, flying in formation, and navigation. They had learned to evaluate the wind by observing the conditions on the ground. They had acquired valuable experience in all types of weather conditions (...) Working with paratroopers, the "flyboys", they had honed their skills during the training manoeuvres and "war-games" in North Carolina. These "war-games" were designed with the objective of pushing the participants and their aircraft to the limit, the crews were also operating with a minimum of sleep and pilot fatigue sometimes reached dangerous levels.*"

In February 1944, while the unit was preparing to leave for England by air, "*the excitement was at its height among the men*", recalls Charles Everett Bullard. " *The big and beautiful brand new C- 47s had up until this time been parked out of sight. Each of us received a plane to which he was personally attributed... I focused my attention on this big, very big and beautiful plane. No words can explain the feeling I felt for it. Undoubtedly, you remember the first time you get into a car, the smell of fresh paint and the smell of the new inside. That was the feeling I had for the first brand new C-47 I saw. It was in perfect condition. I did not know that during the next eighteen months, this airplane and I would become inseparable companions...*"

Like his counterpart John Nagy, Crew Chief of the *Stoy Hora*, Bullard always stayed with his aircraft. The rest of the crew were able to change planes, but not the Crew-Chief.

Crest of the 440th TCG.

We were all afraid to go over the Pacific

On 23 February, the flight itinerary on board 52 new C-47s, left Baer Field to travel the 18 000 kilometres destined for England via South America. The first stop was Puerto Rico. The men did not know their final destination. Would it be the Pacific or could it be Europe ? This information was to be kept secret until they were beyond the continental limits of the United States.

"*When the pilot opened the sealed orders*" recalls Bullard, "*a jubilant cry resounded, we were all afraid of going over the Pacific.*" Charles Everett continues his description of the trip : "*The flight to Belem (Brazil) was the most terrifying part of the whole trip. We flew over terrain where, as far as we could see, dense scrub emerged from water that could hardly have been more than thirty centimetres to one metre deep. You could not help but dread the horror of an engine failure and a forced landing in the horrible mud below us. To stay under the clouds, we were almost on the trees tops, this gave us a very clear vision of what was sprawled out below. If a plane landed in this chaotic landscape, it would have taken days for a rescue team to come to its rescue ...* "

After a long flight over the water towards the Ascension Isles, the 440th TCG successfully crossed the Atlantic Ocean heading in the direction of Africa. On the way it stopped off at Dakar, and then took the Morocco route, to the north. Before landing in Marrakech, Bullard recalls that the C-47 flew across "*the Sahara desert, which seemed from the sky like a place where for nothing on earth would one like to have engine problems and have to land in disaster.*"

The last part of the journey was made inside the combat zone, while most of the dangerous portion of the route was covered in darkness. Bullard goes on to describe this: "*Although not a sign of us had been seen by the enemy, the tension was evident among the men. The term "enemy territory" was sufficient enough to keep us on our guard. The passengers and crew slept very little that night.*"

Finally, on April 26, after a few weeks had passed by on English soil, the 440th was moved to base 463, near Exeter, in the county of Devon. Exeter would be its home for the next five months as well as its point of departure for the invasion of France.

From early March until May 29, the men were subjected to a harsh training program, with the American Airborne units in preparation for the invasion of France. But during their free time they were able enjoy the English countryside, in particular the impressive natural beauty of the town of Torquay, as well as its many fine hotels.

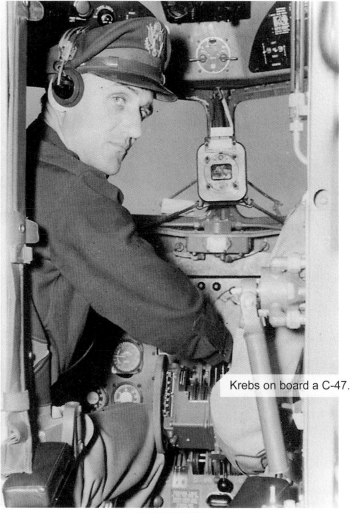

Krebs on board a C-47.

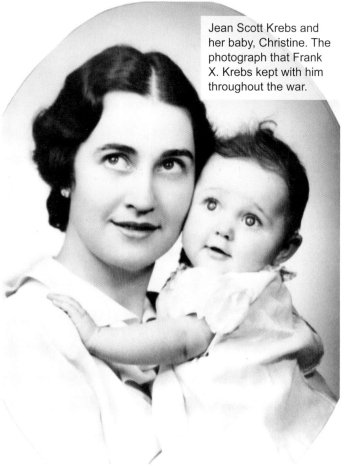

Jean Scott Krebs and her baby, Christine. The photograph that Frank X. Krebs kept with him throughout the war.

Frank X. Krebs.

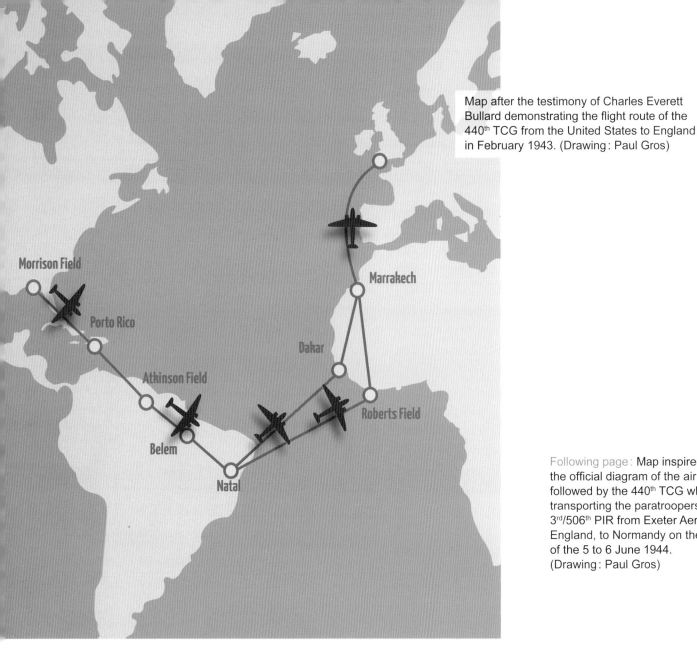

Map after the testimony of Charles Everett Bullard demonstrating the flight route of the 440th TCG from the United States to England in February 1943. (Drawing: Paul Gros)

Morrison Field

Porto Rico

Atkinson Field

Belem

Natal

Marrakech

Dakar

Roberts Field

Following page: Map inspired by the official diagram of the air route followed by the 440th TCG while transporting the paratroopers of the 3rd/506th PIR from Exeter Aerodrome, England, to Normandy on the night of the 5 to 6 June 1944. (Drawing: Paul Gros)

En route to D-Day

Less than a month before D-Day, the 440th participated in Operation "Eagle". Randy Hils describes this exercise like this: "*On May 11 and 12, under the watchful eye of General Dwight D. Eisenhower and Sir Winston Churchill, crews transporting the troops and paratroopers demonstrated with success the awesome power of the airborne forces and of the TCG.*"

He continues: "*The first two operational components of Operation "Neptune" (code name for the Normandy assault phase within the general framework of Operation "Overlord"): the "Albany" (101st) and "Boston" (82nd) operations, were planned as an assault led by two airborne divisions of over 13,000 paratroopers behind German lines, in order to support the amphibious landings the next morning on Utah Beach. Each infantry paratrooper unit had a specific goal in the Norman*

territory. The goal was to place each unit in the proximity of its objectives in a oval area of about 2.5 kilometres wide. This required that each of the 821 aircraft occupy a precise location within the formation. This complex mission needed to be planned in advance and based on a strict time schedule depending on the location of the airdrop zones.

Assembling so many planes in a specific order required precise pilot control, with groups operating to the exact minute, depending on the expected time of arrival and the necessary time for assembling. Missions dropping paratroopers needed to be followed by the arrival of glider missions in the morning. Operation "Neptune" remains unique in the history of war. Never before, or since, has an nocturnal airborne operation of this scale ever been attempted."

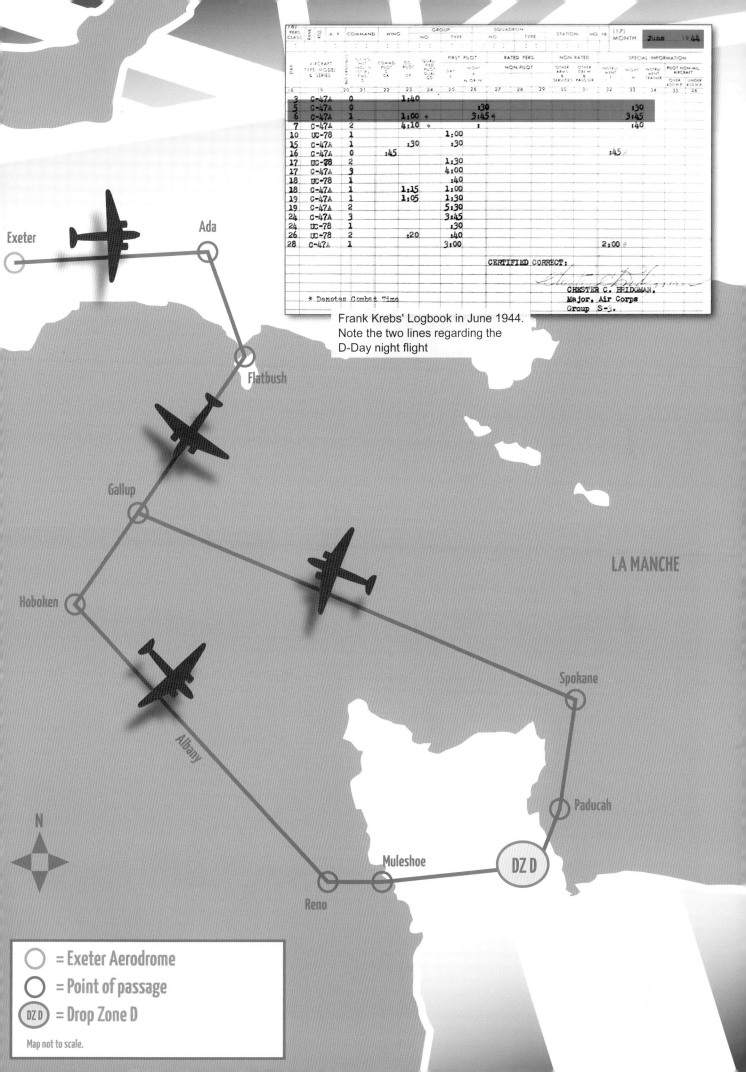

Frank Krebs' Logbook in June 1944.
Note the two lines regarding the
D-Day night flight

* Denotes Combat Time

CERTIFIED CORRECT:

CHESTER C. BRIDGMAN,
Major, Air Corps
Group S-3.

Exeter

Ada

Flatbush

Gallup

Hoboken

Albany

LA MANCHE

Spokane

Paducah

Muleshoe

DZ D

Reno

N

= Exeter Aerodrome

= Point of passage

DZ D = Drop Zone D

Map not to scale.

11:50 p.m., June 5, 1944. The heavily laden C-47 "Stoy Hora" piloted by Lieutenant Colonel Krebs, leaves the runway at Exeter, England. It is the first one of forty-five aircraft belonging to the 440th TCG.

Inside the aircraft, Lieutenant-Colonel Robert L. Wolverton and crew Lieutenant Bobuck from HQ/3rd/506th PIR are in their places, there is also an unexpected passenger in the person of Ward Smith. This war correspondent is following the American forces for the News of the World. Smith, who boarded at the last minute, had the task of retelling the paratroopers' voyage to Normandy.

Charles Everett Bullard explains that "*the 95th, 96th, 97th and 98th squadrons of the 440th TCG would constitute the Serial No.16, the last of the Albany mission, charted to assure the airlift of the 101st Airborne Division. The 3rd/506th PIR, the men of the "Filthy Thirteen", an elite team specialising in demolition and sabotage, and the*

first and third platoons of Company C of the 326th Airborne Engineer Battalion, formed the "combat cargo" of the 440th."

The C-47 Group were about to reconvene to create the largest air armada of all time. Eight hundred twenty-one aircraft had been mobilised to transport 13,000 paratroopers from the 82nd and 101st Airborne Division to Normandy. Bullard remembers that "*the pilots and crews were tense and determined to drop those fighters exactly where they were supposed to go.*"

Randy Hils details this: "*Everything was carefully orchestrated like a complex ballet. Each aircraft in each squadron of each group had an assigned place among the formation, in "V on V", each squadron had a place*

among the group, each group a place assigned within the imposing formation. This needed to facilitate the routing of paratrooper units in a specific order. The base formation had nine planes at the front. Three groups of three C-47s arranged in an inverted "V", constituting in their turn a larger "V" of nine aircraft. The "V on V" formation permitted the pilots to observe the nine small blue position lights of the aircraft in front of them. The blue lights were only visible from behind and above (they indicated the top of the wings and fuselage of the aircraft). Special shields had to be installed on the exhaust to reduce their detection from the ground. Three hundred metres separated each wave of nine aircraft. Four or five groups of nine aircraft constituted a Serial, the specific group generally utilised for the Normandy mission. The observation of the nine small position lights would last for about five hours."

Absolute silence

The flight plan was the fruit of experience gained from previous years. Nothing had been left to chance. Radio silence needed to be absolute. It was the indispensable condition for guaranteeing the security of the operation. Randy Hils adds: *"As flight leader, the Stoy Hora therefore flew at the head of the formation. It carried two experienced navigators. "Rebecca" a transceiver system would enable it to receive the signal sent by the scouting paratroopers fifteen minutes before its arrival in the drop zone. The Stoy Hora was the only aircraft equipped with radar and receivers capable of capturing radio signals sent by the scouts from the drop zone. Strapped to her belly were some containers to be dropped at the same time as the men. Some contained heavy weapons, others ammunition and some had explosives, should they be hit by enemy fire catastrophic results were guaranteed."*

Each of the five successive waves of the 440th TCG needed to fly at an altitude higher than the previous one. This permitted, on the one hand, the planes of each wave to visualise the positioning lights of the lead aircraft, and, secondly, at the time of the jump, it would allow the aircraft who were following to avoid collision with the paratroopers filling the sky at the time of the airdrops.

A magnificent view when everything was going well

Krebs' formation sank into the night above the Channel, in a south-westerly direction, following an indirect trajectory. The Air Force flew with a cross wind to the destination on the Cotentin Peninsula at only 150 meters above the surface of the water in order to avoid the German radar. A minimum safety distance of 30 metres separated the tips of the wings of each aircraft. The 440th TCG was subjected to enemy fire early on as it passed the Channel Islands, but this proved ineffective because it was out of the reach of the German guns.

During the flight, lasting about 1 hour 40 minutes, the roar of the engines deafened the paratroopers who were slumbering in the darkness of the cabin. A lull before the storm of fire and steel that would soon be unleashed...

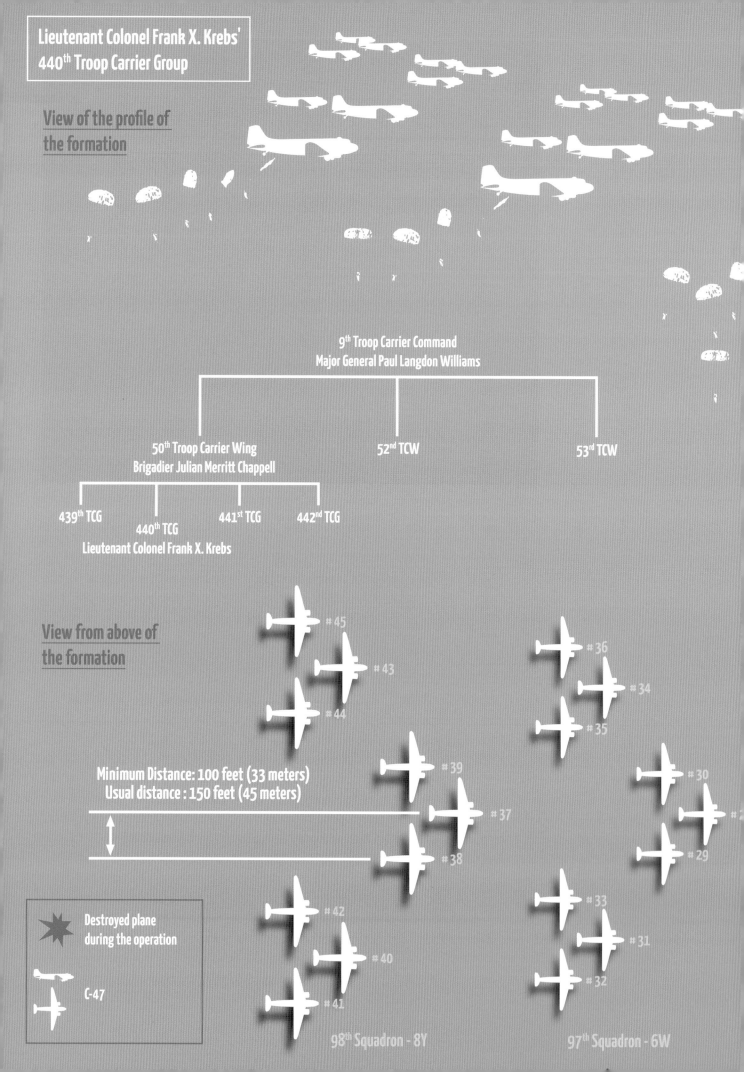

Lieutenant Colonel Frank X. Krebs' 440th Troop Carrier Group

View of the profile of the formation

9th Troop Carrier Command
Major General Paul Langdon Williams

50th Troop Carrier Wing
Brigadier Julian Merritt Chappell

52nd TCW

53rd TCW

439th TCG

440th TCG
Lieutenant Colonel Frank X. Krebs

441st TCG

442nd TCG

View from above of the formation

45
43
44

36
34
35

39
37
38

30
29

Minimum Distance: 100 feet (33 meters)
Usual distance : 150 feet (45 meters)

42
40
41

33
31
32

★ Destroyed plane
during the operation

✈ C-47

98th Squadron - 8Y

97th Squadron - 6W

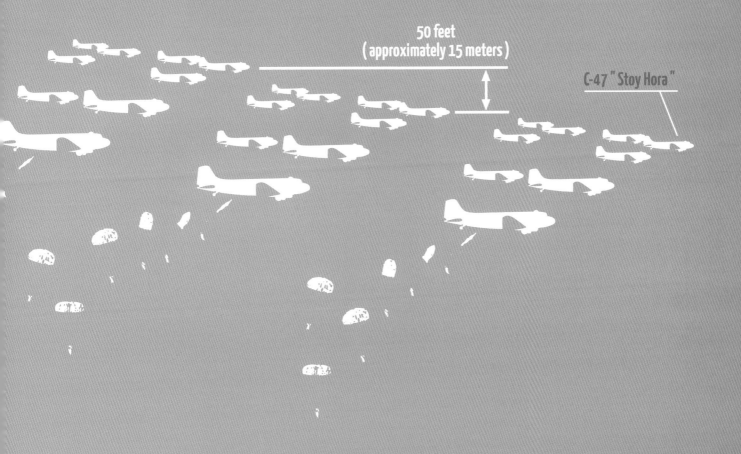

Overview of the 440th TCG on the night of June 6, according to the description given by Randy Hils. (Drawing : Paul Gros)

50 feet
(approximately 15 meters)

C-47 " Stoy Hora "

1000 feet
(approximately 300 meters)

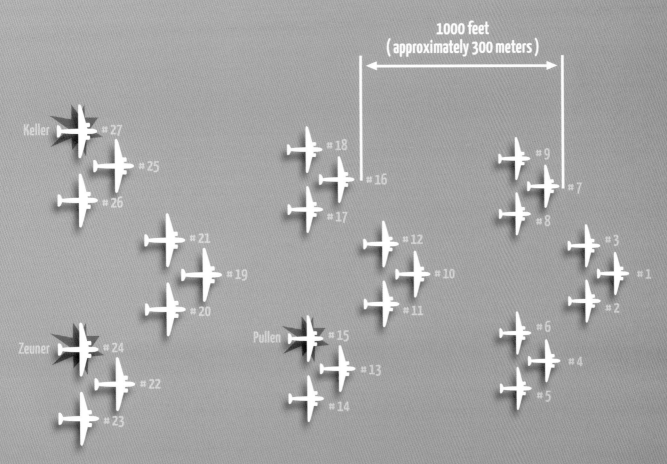

Keller #27
#25
#26

#18
#16
#17

#9
#7
#8

#21
#19
#20

#12
#10
#11

#3
#1
#2

Zeuner #24
#22
#23

Pullen #15
#13
#14

#6
#4
#5

96th Squadron - 6Z

95th Squadron - 9X

HQ Squadron

War correspondent Ward Smith circulated his notebook among the paratroopers. They signed their names in it and, in the case of some, their addresses with a few personal words. Corporal Jack Harrison gave Smith a pack of cigarettes. He thought that after the drop, left alone on the silent and empty plane, the reporter would need them for the long trip back to England.

Charles Everett Bullard had a great deal of luck. He was on board the No.43 plane piloted by Leonard Thompson of the 98th Squadron. The C-47 was leading the "V" formation situated to the left of the last wave of the 440th TCG. On board, a team from Company C of the 326th Airborne Engineer Battalion had taken their places. He still re-calls the incredible vision of the armada that he marvelled over during the flight from the astrodome: "*A bubble plastic shaped like a helmet, but a little larger, which provided a 360° panoramic view of the plane. Believe me, it was a magnificent view when eve-rything was going well.*"

C-47s from the 440th TCG flying across the English Channel covering some of the boats from view. (Drawing and colour: Christophe Esquerré)

Randy Hils says that the team of scouts, made up of hand picked paratroopers, needed to land 30 minutes before the arrival of the group: "*Twenty C-47s carrying the scouts were already in the air. The job of the scouts was to identify and to mark the drop zones on the Co-tentin peninsula, with the "Eureka" radio beacons and to illuminate the "T" lamps that would guide the mass of approaching aircraft throughout the last kilometres before reaching the drop zone. The scouts were an elite unit, a group of specially trained paratroopers and volunteer crews. Despite the problems, with the help of the "GEE" British radar, all of the scout teams were close enough to the parachute drop zone to fulfil their mission. However, thick fog and skirmishes with the enemy prevented some scouts from completely fulfilling the task. With only 30 minutes to set up radio beacons and lights, some scouts were immediately taken under fire from the enemy. In Drop Zone D, the scouts found themselves caught up in a "hornet's nest" full of Ger-mans. They were successful in disposing of the radio beacons but not the "T" lamps for guiding the aircraft.*"

Unbeknownst to Krebs and his pilots, a series of obs-tacles threatened to thwart the careful preparations for the aerial assault... On the approach to the Normandy coast, the 440th in effect met with a sheet of cloud that rose up in its path like an ominous barrier. Since no weather plane had been sent in advance, the pilots were not to know that a massive bank of cloud was looming on the horizon, formed from the mist rising up from the ground. With a maximum altitude limited to 16 000 feet (about 5000 meters), the C-47 pilots were not able to fly above the bad weather. They were often forced to fly underneath the atmospheric perturbations or run the risk of breaking up the formation, as Randy Hils clarifies.

Three aircraft hit in full flight

Krebs quickly identified the danger and changed alti-tude, bringing the 440th underneath the clouds. He had studied the topography of the terrain beforehand and knew he was able to lead his group safely by flying lower down. Completely dependent on their leader, the pilots who were following the *Stoy Hora* conserved the cohesion of the formation, identifying each other by the faint blue lights fixed on the back of the planes.

The success of the paratroopers mission that Krebs was leading into combat now depended on his ability, on his sense of direction, and on the long months of training to which he and his men had been subjected. The French coast was visible now, and the planes levelled to the correct altitude to prepare for the drop.

On the ground, the Germans were ready to welcome the invaders. They had identified the drop zones around strategic objectives and had concentrated troops, searchlights, machine guns and anti-aircraft canons.

The Cotentin Peninsula is only thirty-three kilometres wide. At a cruising speed of 225 km / h, it took the C-47s less than ten minutes to cross it, before they were again over the English Channel.

Over the last ten kilometres coming up to Drop Zone D, the path became even tougher when near miss explosions damaged the aircraft. The 440th crossed an intense barrage of anti-aircraft guns, machine guns and light arms. The bright search lights and the bright phosphorus flares that swept the sky blinded some of the pilots, annihilating their precious night vision. The wind blew in gusts of 35 to 55 km / h, well beyond the speed considered safe for combat jumps which was 28 km / h.

Since the orders given to the pilots were to drop their troops as "close to the combat zone" as possible, if the drop zone was missed on the first crossing, pilots in many groups made several crossings in an extremely perilous approach, striving to deliver their troops to their goal. Some of them paid with their lives and with that of their crews.

During the crossing of the peninsula from west to east, three aircraft were hit. In a desperate effort, the pilots of these sacrificed their lives so that some of the paratroopers were able to extract themselves from the flaming

aircraft before they finally crashed along with the crew. The *Donna Mae* came to a tragic end by falling on the commune of Magneville, resulting in the death of four crew members and the eighteen paratroopers situated on board.

A farm building set alight by the Germans

Slowly, the formation reduced its speed from 240 to 180 km / h. The paratroopers had risen from their seats as the red light came on. Only four minutes remained before the jump...

Wolverton's men hooked on the carabiners (metal belts loops) from the static line cable of the aircraft, checked their equipment and that of the comrade directly in front of them, and signalled that they were ready by yelling the count from the back to the front of the hold : "16 OK , 15 OK , 14 OK ... 3 OK 2 OK 1 OK " ...

The C-47s were being shaken by explosions from anti-aircraft shells. Expecting the lamp to turn green giving the signal to jump, loaded up like mules, weighed down by all the equipment they carried, the paratroopers were unbalanced by the brusque pilot manoeuvres needed to escape anti-aircraft search-lights, scouring the night with their sharp beams.

On land, the Germans were in the throws of burning a farm building that they had doused in carburant. The firelight that resulted illuminated the whole drop zone, cutting through the black sky was the silhouette of the light grey underbelly of the C-47s and of the paratroopers.

It was 01:40 hours on the morning of 6 June 1944.

With the deluge of gunfire continuing to intensify in the approach to Drop Zone D, the drop zone normally assigned to the 3rd/506th PIR near to Angoville-au-Plain, Colonel Krebs finally gave the order to release the paratroopers who were now impatient to leave the aircraft as fast as possible. Within seconds, the *Stoy Hora* was emptied of its human cargo above the village of Saint-Côme-du-Mont.

Lead by Wolverton, their leader, who jumped first, the men of 3rd/506th PIR had filled their camouflage nets as the Normandy sky lit up like fireworks. Lieutenant Bobuck left the plane last. Nobody suspected the massacre about to begin within seconds. It is a sort of irony that this area, located a little south of the DZ D, was the best defended in the sector...

At the moment of diving, the paratroopers were caught up in a fireworks display which, in addition to being spectacular, would also prove fatal to a large number of them. Rapidly, the men, weighed down by their weapons and equipment, descended towards the Normandy soil, even a few seconds must have seemed like an eternity as they were suspended between heaven and earth and surrounded by the hellish fire.

Some found themselves entangled in the trees, others trying to cut themselves loose from their parachutes, were hit by German bullets while they were engaged in cutting their lines to remove the harness. Others were immediately spotted, disarmed and captured, if not summarily executed.

New mission over Normandy on June 7

Already, the silhouettes of the C-47s were being illuminated by the reflection of the moon as they moved off toward the horizon, in the coastal direction. The *Stoy Hora* initiated a slow climb to reach an altitude of 1000 metres, for her return to England. But the mission for Krebs' men was not finished. Upon landing, John Nagy, Charles Everett Bullard and all the Crew Chiefs needed to organise the refuelling of the aircraft, to look around and assess the damage and to prepare for the next trip. The C-47 bore the marks of the gauntlet they had just run. Miraculously, no crew member had been injured.

While the pilots and crew were participating in the debriefing and taking a comforting swig of alcohol, the damaged units would be assigned to the technical staff on the ground in order to prepare for the next mission that would surely come at day break. Indeed, the 440th would need to return above Normandy on June 7, as part of operation Memphis, to replenish the men of the 101st Airborne Division engaged on the ground in fierce combat. Krebs and his men would face enemy fire once again, but this time it was daylight and the surprise effect would not work. The Germans were waiting for them on a firmer footing.

Alone in the dark and silent cabin of the *Stoy Hora* with Sergeant Nagy, Ward Smith meditated by contemplating the pack of cigarettes given to him by Jack Harrison. He decided to keep the cigarettes to give them back to Harris when he returned home to the United States. On his return to the camp, he wrote his article and recorded his story on tape for posterity. In his article in the News of the World magazine one week later, entitled "I saw them jump to destiny" Smith defined the moment of the jump with these words: "*These men, so young, so brave, were left to their destiny.*"

He was far from imagining what dramatic conditions they encountered...

Notebook that the BBC reporter Ward Smith circulated to the paratroopers in Bobuck's stick during the flight to Normandy. One detail deserves mention, the man who signed the bottom of the last page "Sgt Nagy, New Jersey" had not belonged to the 3rd/506th PIR. Initially mistakenly identified as an naval artillery observer, this mysterious man was supposed to have taken the place normally reserved for Ed Shames next to Wolverton, and he could have died at his side, suspended from another tree at Saint-Côme-du-Mont. This puzzle was finally solved by Charles Everett Bullard, who confirmed that the Crew Chief of the *Stoy Hora* was in fact his counterpart John Nagy. Taking flight in the cargo with the paratroopers it was therefore natural that he also signed Ward Smith's notebook, mentioning his rank, name and city of residence.

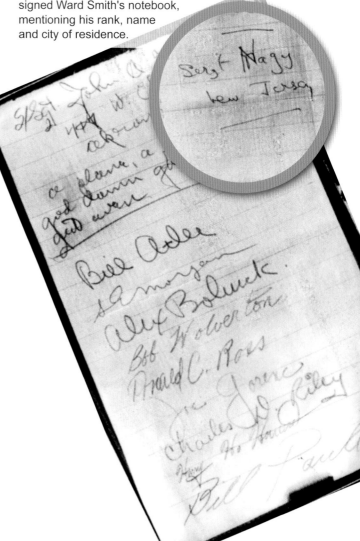

Just a week after his return, Ward Smith published the article entitled "I saw them jump to destiny" in the News of the World. Here is the full text.

"So closely had the secret of D-Day been preserved that not all the flying crews themselves knew the signal had been given till they took off.

The paratroops had been in barbed-wire enclosures for some days. No one had any chance to talk.

The previous day I had flown into London and back on urgent business. Immediately on my return I was summoned to a squadron headquarters to sleep.
But they didn't show me my room. Instead they led me right out to the airfield, to the first of a line of waiting planes. "*This is It!*" they remarked.

It had come at last - just like that....

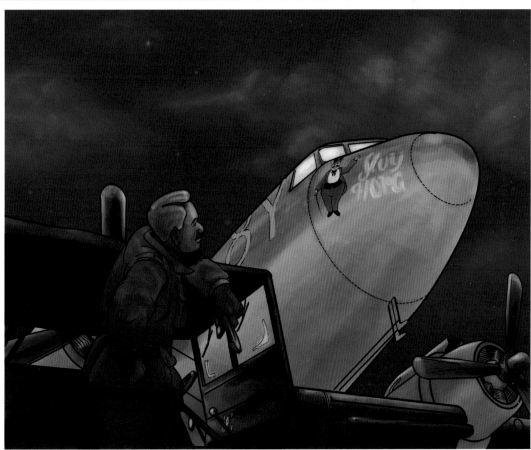

As I climbed aboard, paratroops, steel-helmeted, black-faced, festooned from head to foot, were in their planes in the bucket-seats lining each side of the fuselage.

The co-pilot, Major Cannon, was reading a historic message from General Eisenhower. It spoke of the "*Great Crusade*" and ended: "*Let us beseech the blessing of Almighty God on this noble undertaking.*"

As the door slanged to on us, sitting there in the dusk, we realized that we had suddenly passed from one world to another. Perhaps that was partly the effect of the all-red lights on the plane. They made our faces look slightly blue. They turned the red tips of our cigarettes white. I think that perhaps all of us had rather a sinking feeling in the pit of the stomach. But that didn't last long. Somehow we seemed to leave it behind on the ground. Almost before we realized it we were off. Here and there lights, friendly lights, winked at us. Other planes, their red and green wing lights twinkling cheerfully, fell into close formation behind to left and right.

As everyone adjusted parachute harness, flak suits, and Mae Wests, our mood brightened to a spate of banter. "*Say*" someone sang out suddenly, "*what's the date?*" "*I'll feel kinda dumb down there if some guy asks me and I get it wrong.*"

We laughed uproariously at things like that - the smallest things, the silliest things.

We exchanged cigarettes and we talked on - but somehow never about things that mattered.

Down below a beacon flashed out a code letter. We made a sharp turn over to the coast. Then our roof lights, our wing lights, and the lights of all the fleet behind abruptly flicked out. We were heading out to sea.
We fell silent, just sat and watched the darkened ghosts sailing along behind us in the twilight.

I noticed a red sign on the jump door, just one word:

"Think"

I tried to remember what the jump master had told me: "*If you have to bale out, don't forget to pull this tag to strip off the flak suit*"; "*when you jump remember to count to two before you pull the rip cord*"; "*if you hit the sea you MUST unbuckle this 'chute clip here before you pull the tassel to inflate the Mae West, or it'll choke you.*"

while I was reflecting that I was certain to forget something, shore lights flashed in the distance. We could just make out land on the horizon under a glimmer of moon. The coast of France....

This was it - the Great Adventure everyone had lived for and worked for so long and so hard. I hated to see it; and yet it thrilled me.

Hitler's Europe.

Those lights went out. A flare went up. Had they seen us? Had they heard us? The moon silvered the fleet behind.

"*A pity someone said we were going in here*", one of the paratroopers remarked suddenly. We knew what he meant.
He was talking of that extraordinary report that reached America some hours before that the Allies were already landing in France. Well, as it turned out, it was right. We were going into Northern France. Up here, now that lives were at stake, someone's idiocy didn't seem amusing.

We took a sharp turn towards the land. And here I must pay tribute to the planning. So cunning was our routing, so many our twists and turns, that at no time till we reached our objective could the enemy have gained an inkling as to just were we were bound.

The land slid by, silent and grey. And still nothing happened. Some of the paratroopers chorused "Put that pistol down, Momma" and "For Me and My Girl"

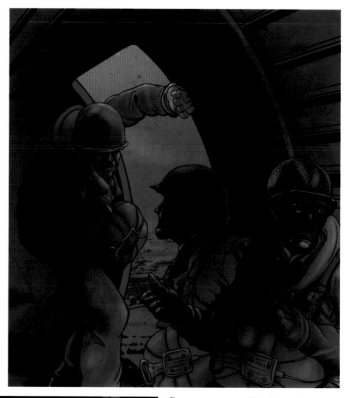

Someone called out:

"*TEN MINUTES TO GO!*".

I shall never forget the scene up there in those last fateful minutes, those long lines of motionless, grim-faced young men burdened like pack-horses so that they could hardly stand unaided. Just waiting...

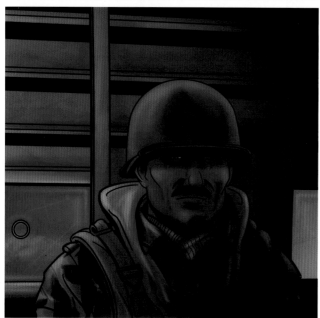

They looked so young, and on the verge of the unknown, and somehow so sad. Most sat with eyes closed as the seconds ticked by. They seemed to be asleep, but I could see lips moving wordlessly. I wasn't consciously thinking of anything in particular, but suddenly I found the phrase "*Thy rod and Thy staff*" moving through my mind again and again. Just that and no more. It was all very odd.

Then things began to happen.
Below we saw fires on all sides. Our bombers had done their work well.

Corporal Jack Harrison of Phoenix, Arizona, leaned over and thrust a packet of cigarettes in my hand.
"*You might need them on the way back*" he said.

I said, "*What about you?*"
He just shrugged. Then he lined up
with the others.

The jump door opened, letting in a dull
red glare from the fires below. The time
had come. We were over the drop zone.
I wish I could play up that moment,
but there was nothing to indicate that
this was the supreme climax.

"Just a whistling that lasted for a few seconds - and those men, so young, so brave, had gone to their destiny.

I'd expected them to whoop battle-cries, to raise the roof in that last fateful moment. But not one of them did. They just stepped silently out into the red night, leaving behind only the echo of the songs they had been singing."

"Then we got it. The flak and tracer came up, from all sides. Through the still-open door in the side of the plane I could see it forming a blazing arch over us - an arch that lasted for minutes on end, so close it seemed that we could not escape."

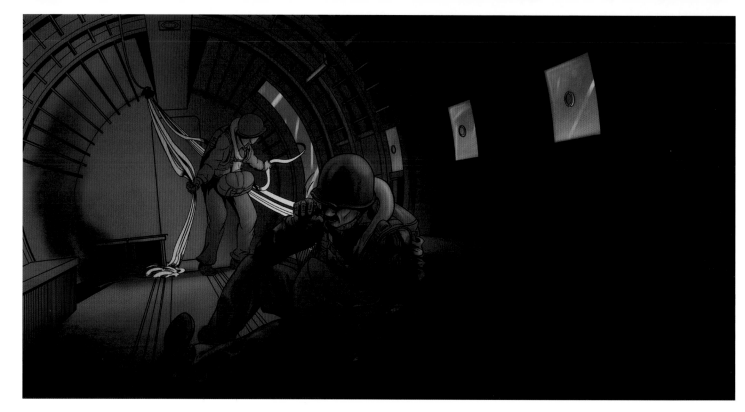

It felt very lonely up there then in that empty C 47. I think I sat on the floor. About the only thing I can be sure of is that I was bathed in perspiration.

I knew we were a sitting target. We didn't have a gun or any armour-plate. Our only safeguard was our racing engines and the cool-headedness and skill of the pilot, Colonel Krebs, as he twisted and dived.

I thought their fighters would be after us. But, fortunately, not a single one showed up from start to finish.
Well, we came back. Three of Colonel Krebs' fleet didn't.
"*We were lucky*", said the colonel as we streaked for home.

Standing behind him in the cockpit, you could see fleets of planes passing in each direction, guided by beacons on the water in a perfectly organized system of traffic control. The sea seemed full of ships. Soon the first seaborne forces would be going in...

We came back. Our paratroopers hadn't - yet. At the moment, they're too busy to tell their story. Just in case Corporal Harrison happens to read this, I'd like him to know that I'm keeping his cigarettes for him. Perhaps he might like a smoke on the way home. But if he can spare them I'd like to keep them always.

Back at the base, as we ate, two young officers walked in to breakfast and flipped over the morning papers. "So the Allies have taken Rome" they remarked. "*Well, it shouldn't be long now before the invasion starts.*"

They didn't know, yet...

Ward Smith"

Of all the component units of the 101st Airborne Division, the 3rd battalion of 506th regiment had the highest proportion of victims, not less than ninety-three killed and seventy-five prisoners.

The stick on board the *Stoy Hora* was particularly tested: five of the sixteen paratroopers on board lost their lives in Normandy. The survivors had all been captured, some escaped, four of them were injured. Despite these losses, the mission assigned to the 3rd/506th PIR was fulfilled. Even though very few men reached the bridges at Brévands these managed to remain in the hands of American paratroopers until the joining with the U.S. 4th Infantry Division.

Of the sixteen paratroopers from Lieutenant Bobuck's group who left England on June 5, only five were able to take part in the follow up operation in Holland, code-named Market Garden, in September 1944.

Forty veterans from the 3rd/506th PIR would respond to Lieutenant Colonel Robert Lee Wolverton's invitation after the war. On 6 June 1946, they met at the Muelbach Hotel in Kansas City. One of the men read aloud Wolverton's prayer, some of them were crying, and Kathleen Wolverton received the Legion of Merit, the decoration posthumously awarded to her husband, from General Taylor.

The Legion of Merit

Reunion of the 3rd/506th PIR at Muelbach Hotel, Kansas City, Missouri, in June 1946. In the first row, the 7th man from the left is Ed Shames. Kathleen Wolverton is at the centre of the group in a black skirt. Ray Calandrella is in the last row, the third man from the right.

The first man on the left is Ed Shames, the second man on the right is Ray Calandrella.

the jump of his battalion in Normandy. For three days his body hung from a tree at Saint-Côme-du-Mont. At dawn on June 9, the American paratroopers, who had taken control of the village, finally cut him down. The awful news spread amongst the men, desperate to know what had become of their leader since the drop. It was a shock for everyone.

Exeter, England, June 4, 1944.

John A. Rinehart was born on April 4, 1924 in the state of Maryland. Single, without children, John resided in Baltimore, Maryland, and worked in the paint varnishing industry. He enlisted at Baltimore on March 3, 1943. As with all of his comrades, he volunteered for the duration of the War or other emergencies, with the possibility of an additional six months if the President of the United States, or any other person in accordance with the law so decided. John, who held the position of *pigeon man* (he transported the carrier pigeons) had, it seems, been shot in the DZ (Drop Zone) as he tried to free himself from his parachute harness.

On June 6, 1984, in a speech to mark the 40th anniversary of the landings, President Ronald Reagan honoured the memory of Wolverton: "*Something else helped the men on D-Day: Their firm belief that Providence would have a very strong influence in the events that were to take place here, that God was an ally in this great cause. And so, on the eve of the invasion, when Colonel Wolverton asked his paratroopers to kneel with him in prayer he told them: "Do not look down but up with faces raised to the sky to see God and ask his blessing for what we are going to do."*"

The death of Wolverton succinctly embodies the verse of John, chapter 15: "*There is no greater love than to lay down his life for his friends.*"

The memory of this remarkable man was still vivid after the landings. According to Ed Shames, "*There was no one like him.*"

Jack W. Harrison was born on August 2, 1921 in Michigan. Single, in charge of a family, Jack resided at Maricopa County, Arizona. He had acquired comprehensive driving qualifications that enabled him to drive all kinds of vehicles: buses, taxis, trucks, tractors, etc. Jack enlisted in Phoenix, Arizona on September 16, 1942. Wounded in the stomach on

Fort Bragg, USA, July 1943.

D-Day, taken prisoner by the Germans, he died June 25, 1944 in some agony. He never had the opportunity to smoke the cigarettes he had offered Ward Smith, the journalist in the hold of the *Stoy Hora*. The packet was finally opened, and the cigarettes smoked many years later, after the war, in a hotel somewhere in London by William Pauli, Ward Smith and Joseph Beyrle (a PIR 3rd/506th veteran, Joe had landed on the steeple of the Church of Saint-Côme-du-Mont before being made prisoner).

Killed in action

Robert Lee Wolverton was born on October 5, 1914 in the United States, at Elkins in Randolph County, West Virginia. Married, father of a little boy, he died in France still in his parachute harness on June 6, 1944 at 1:40 hours in the morning, in the seconds following

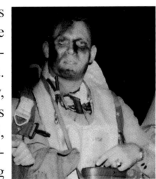

Exeter, England, June 5, 1944.

Anthony M. Wincenciak Jr. was on born October 4, 1924 in the state of New York. Single, with no children, he lived in the county of Chautauqua, New York, and enlisted at Buffalo, New York on May 20, 1943. He was killed in Normandy on 20 June 1944. He is buried at the cemetery in Saint Hedwig, Dunkirk, in the Chautauqua section.

Exeter, England, June 4, 1944.

jumped from airplane No.2, immediately followed by three marine artillery observers. Grant and the three men suffered the same fate as Wolverton. They were all killed on landing).

The bodics of Wolverton, Rinehart, Harrison and Wincenciak were repatriated by the United States Government at the request of their families. Wolverton is buried on his home territory in the historic cemetery of the Military Academy at West Point, New York, among his valorous compatriots.

Exeter, England, June 4, 1944.

William H. Atlee was born in 1914 in Iowa. Divorced, no children, he lived in Lee County, Iowa where he worked in the accounting profession. Enlisted voluntarily on December 8, 1941, "Bill" joined the infantry at Camp Dodge Herrold, Iowa, on September 24, 1942. He died on June 6, during a reconnaissance patrol, on a small road located to the south of Saint-Côme-du-Mont, he is the only man in Bobuck's group who still rests in Normandy. "Bill" is buried at the American cemetery at Colleville-Sur-Mer, among the 9387 white marble crosses, just a few meters from Major Grant, the second officer of 3rd/506th PIR (Grant

Wounded and prisoners of war

Doctor **Stanley E. Morgan** and Nurse **Thomas E. Newell**, of the medical team attached to the 3rd/506th, were injured during the jump and captured shortly after landing in the village of Saint-Côme-du-Mont. They nevertheless valiantly completed their medical duty to the wounded of all nationalities and of affected French civilians.

Tom Newell, seriously wounded in the leg and foot on D-Day, was liberated in Normandy, then evacuated to England. Captain Morgan Stanley, was a native of New

Stanley E. Morgan, Exeter, England, June 4, 1944.

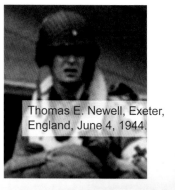

Thomas E. Newell, Exeter, England, June 4, 1944.

June 6th 16:00 hours. The prisoners have been lined up by their captives in front of "Stalag B " They receive their first meal of the day, a "clear soup".

Orleans, Louisiana. A surgeon, graduate of the medical school at Louisiana State University, he sprained an ankle during the jump. He was awarded the Purple Heart. He was liberated in Normandy on June 8, 1944. He returned to the 3rd/506th PIR, jumped again in Holland and was captured again at Opheusden on 5 October of the same year. Detained at the Obermaßfeld 1249 hospital (*Stalag 9C*), Thuringia, Germany, until the end of the war, he was finally liberated on 8 May 1945. Morgan Stanley died in 2002.

An article by an unknown author concerning the medical history of the 3rd/506th PIR in Normandy, sent in by Robert R. Webb, Jr. (son of veteran Robert R. Webb, Sr. of HQ/3rd/506th PIR), gives us a few more details about his brave commitment in Normandy : "*After a short interview, Captain Morgan was conducted to a position in the German infirmary located at Saint-Come-du-Mont, where he courageously and fearlessly administered first aid and emergency surgical care to great number of American and German victims who had been taken there. With the help of a German doctor and military from the ranks, he worked continuously for three days in the greatest danger, under threat from both the German's desire for revenge and Allied artillery. The town was besieged and was finally taken on the afternoon of June 8 1944, thus liberating Morgan. Through his heroic actions and utter disregard for danger he had become a source of encouragement for many wounded American paratroopers who had been rounded up and entrusted to his good care. He had succeeded as much by his diplomatic efforts as by his energy in directing the German evacuation of the seriously injured allied soldiers and at the same time, despite lack of available resources, maintained a tour de force in caring for those with minor injuries until the arrival of the Americans. The injured unanimously praised him, and*

he left a great impression on Germans captured later during the Normandy campaign. Morgan once again proved his disregard for danger and dedication when he volunteered to drive many of the Allied casualties to Saint-Lô in a German ambulance. The roads at that time were under fire from artillery bombardment and allied aircraft, which made the trip extremely dangerous, especially in the vicinity of Carentan. The trip to Saint- Lô (which was not liberated until several weeks later) also earned Morgan the distinction of being the first of the American invasion force to have penetrated so far into enemy lines."

Lieutenant Alex Bobuck enlisted on September 26, 1940 in Miami, Florida. Wounded and captured on

Regimental Command Post at Angoville, France, June 8, 1944 .

D-Day, he collaborated with Captain Morgan at the First Aid station at Saint-Côme-du-Mont. He managed to make the Germans believe he was a "sanitary agent" capable of handling the confusing administrative questions being posed. He escaped on June 10 and was dropped in Holland, where he was wounded again. He participated at the siege of Bastogne, as well as the follow up operations in Alsace-Lorraine, the Ruhr and Austria. Bobuck died in 1961.

William L. Pauli was born in Washington in 1921. He lived in Pondera County, Montana. Single, without children, he exercised the profession of tinsmith, coppersmith and sheet metal worker, before enlisting on August 27, 1942 in Butte, Montana. After being wounded and taken prisoner, he was liberated and repatriated.

Exeter, England, June 4, 1944.

Exeter, England, June 4, 1944.

Joseph F. Gorenc was born on April 24, 1923 in Sheboygan County, in the state of Wisconsin. Single, with no children, he enlisted in Milwaukee, Wisconsin on December 8, 1941 and joined the infantry on 1 October 1942. Captured

on D-Day, he escaped in July 1944 from a column of prisoners, and rejoined the U.S. Army. After the war, Joe started his own business with the two thousand dollars that he won in a game of cards played just before the invasion. He asked his friend, Sergeant Ed Shames to safeguard his money for him while in England. Ed saw no place safer than the Mills family home where he was staying. Unfortunately, this veteran who survived the war, died tragically in an industrial accident on 30 October 1957. He is buried in his hometown, at Greendale Cemetery.

Jesse R. Cross, Charles D. Riley, Harry H. Howard and John A. Taormina were less fortunate. They remained prisoners of war until 1945.

Jesse R. Cross was born in 1924 in Texas. Single, no children, Jesse, who was a farmer enlisted in Dallas, Texas on May 11, 1943 . He was wounded in Normandy.

Exeter, England, June 4, 1944.

Exeter, England, June 4, 1944.

Charles D. Riley was born in 1924 in the state of Wisconsin, Milwaukee. Single, with no children, he enlisted at Milwaukee on December 8, 1941 and joined the Infantry on October 6 1942.

John A. Taormina was a native of Ohio. He was detained and captured with Charles Riley, at *Stalag 3C* Alt Drewitz in the state of Brandenburg - Prussia, Germany.

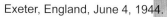

Exeter, England, June 4, 1944.

Exeter, England, June 4, 1944.

Harry H. Howard was born in 1924, in the State of California at Sacramento County. Single, without children, he worked in a service station as a parking lot manager. Harry enlisted on December 8, 1941 in San Francisco, California, and joined the infantry on September 9, 1942. Taken prisoner, he was detained at *Stalag 4B* at Muehlberg on Elba.

June 6, 14:00 hours, *Stalag B.* Taormina, Ross, Riley.

Donald Clifton Ross was born in 1921 in California, San Francisco. Single, with no children, Don taught construction and manual professions and enlisted in San Francisco on August 30, 1942. On D-Day, he jumped from the *Stoy Hora* in the second position,

Exeter, England, June 4, 1944.

just after Colonel Wolverton. He never had the opportunity to put the training he had received at Camp Toccoa into practice, though, fortunately, he narrowly escaped death after the landing. While German soldiers were surrounding him and preparing to summarily execute him, a German officer intervened in a moment of providence. This officer had a brother captured by the Americans and insisted that the rules of the Geneva Convention must be complied with. Don remained a prisoner of war until his liberation in April 1945. He died in March 2004.

Exeter, England, June 4, 1944.

Raymond E. Calandrella was born on November 10, 1923 in the state of Connecticut, New Haven County. Single, without children, Ray was an industrial employee. He enlisted in Hartford, Connecticut on 8 December 1941 and joined the Infantry on September 17, 1942. Captured on D-Day, after a brief shoot out that claimed the life of one of his friends, he escaped in August and rejoined the 3rd/506th PIR towards the end of the campaign in Holland. On November 21, 2011, David Baranowski, the local parish priest where Ray Callendrella had lived, responded with decency and respect with regard to a few questions concerning Ray, much of which can be summarised in these few lines: Although the prospect of killing men in battle was contrary to his Christian faith, Ray Calandrella wanted to do his duty as a citizen to defend his country and support the persecuted Christians of Europe. He believed that Christians were endangered everywhere in the world, as prisoners of the Nazi regime. Beyond his patriotic conscience, he also wanted to defend peace in the world. Calandrella Ray enlisted in the paratroopers because he found this newly created unit exciting, exhilarating and, as such, he would have the opportunity to excel. "*He was a very devoted and very humble soldier.*

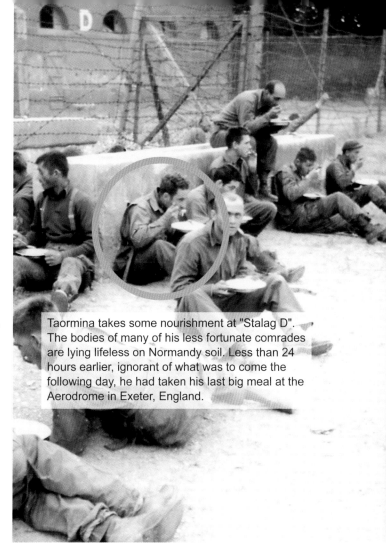

Taormina takes some nourishment at "Stalag D". The bodies of many of his less fortunate comrades are lying lifeless on Normandy soil. Less than 24 hours earlier, ignorant of what was to come the following day, he had taken his last big meal at the Aerodrome in Exeter, England.

He was not proud " remembers Ed Shames. Some of his comrades thinking that this fervent Catholic was too nice to be a paratrooper, made quips about him. The cruellest joked that he was a Nazi spy! He did not like violence, however, and spoke little of the war, in fact he saw little combat. He was taken prisoner twice. The first time on D-Day, shortly after the drop, and then at the Battle of the Bulge. When he was released, they offered to let him return home but he refused, decided to stay and go on until the end.

Father David described Ray as a very religious and profound man, he went to Mass every day and sometimes attended more than one Mass a day! At the end of his life Ray, suffered from cancer of the bladder and had become blind. Even so, Father David never heard him complain when he went to visit him in hospital! Father David shared a treasured keepsake from when he visited Ray in hospital a few days before his death: "*Promise me you'll pray for me still, after my death, and I will die in peace*", has asked the father.

Ray died on 8 July 2005. He rests in peace at Beaverdale Memorial Park Cemetery in New Haven.

Forty-five aircraft from the 440th TCG took part in the nocturnal mission on D-Day. The skill and courage of the pilots enabled the drops that took place here to be among the most accurate performed on the Cotentin Peninsula. On 7 June, the group successfully parachuted equipment, ammunition, food and medicine to the airborne troops.

Losses from the 440th TCG on June 6, 1944

The crew of the *Stoy Hora* returned safe and sound to England. But the 440th had lost three aircraft and their crews and many other aircraft had been damaged.

Shortly after reaching the French coast, the *Donna Mae* from the 95th Squadron, piloted by Lieutenant Ray B. Pullen, suffered catastrophic damage. Randy Hils recounts: "*Finally, the pilot made a last-ditch effort to avoid the farm buildings before the fatal landing that cost the lives of the entire crew as well as the paratroopers on board ... In the last kilometres before the Drop Zone,*

The commemorative site at Magneville.

the 440th lost two additional aircraft from the 96th Squadron due to enemy fire. Both were damaged over the Channel: aircraft No.914 piloted by Sub-Lieutenant R. Alton Keller and aircraft No.733, piloted by Sub-Lieutenant William H. Zeuner."

On the night of August 14 to 15 1944, the six crew members of the *Stoy Hora* would be reunited once again for D-Day, on board the aircraft as part of Operation Anvil Dragoon, namely the Allied landings in Provence. On this occasion, the C-47 would drop

American paratroopers in the region of Muy, about twenty kilometres south of Draguignan.

In September 1944, Krebs and his men from the 440th also participated in Operation Market Garden in Holland. During the course of this mission, the aircraft that Colonel Krebs was flying, the *Miss Yank*, was hit. The crew had to bail out with parachutes from the burning plane and the men landed in enemy territory. Bullard said that forty-five days later, five members of the crew from the *Miss Yank* managed to rejoin the Allied lines, these were Colonel Krebs, Major Cannon, Lieutenant Arnold, Chief Sergeant Bill Quick and Chief Sergeant Broga (Crew Chief of the *Miss Yank*). But Lieutenant Sullivan was less fortunate. Having fallen into the hands of the Germans he spent the rest of the war in a prison camp.

The men of the 440th participated in other operations until the end of the war, including Bastogne and the crossing of the Rhine. Many of them would never return.

The pilots who transported troops suffered criticisms from the writer Stephen E. Ambrose in his book D-Day. In the heat of the action, some paratroopers had been led to believe that the pilots of their planes were irresponsible. In his book Little One and His Guardian Angel, Bullard reasserts the truth: "*The pilot would not have time to explain to the soldiers in the back of the plane that he was trying to avoid some of their comrades who had surged in front of them.*"

To finally do the most elementary justice to his comrades in the 440th, Bullard admits that, like everyone else in life, they experienced fear, but they did what was needed to be done. They attended training at all hours of the day and night, and were trained to fly in all kinds of weather conditions, even in the worst weather. They had even been put through exercises that were very similar to actual war conditions with tracer bullet being fired by the U.S. Navy on the coast of North Carolina. He added: *"It would have been nice if we had had weapons on bord, but this would have forced us to carry a smaller number of soldiers due to the extra weight. As for our fuel tanks, they did not have the advantage of bullet-proofing or self-sealing."*

The *Miss Yank* in distress, after a plastic model made by John Agnew, on which he applied a Nose Art sticker and insignia designs taken from photo archives. (Drawing Paul Gros)

Return to civilian life

Bullard also quotes the message from Colonel Julian M. Chappell, commander of the 50th Troop Carrier Wing: *"I want to express my deepest gratitude through you, to each officer and enlisted man in your unit who by their dedication to duty have reached the highest degree of effectiveness deployed in this operation."* And he said that at the end of the war, Brigadier General Williams, Commander of the IX Troop Carrier Command, had received a warm letter welcomed by everyone, on behalf of the Commander in Chief General Dwight David Eisenhower, which ended with these words: *"You have written a page in the history of the Air Force and the cooperation with the allies that will live forever."*

The greatest proof of the performance of the Group on the ground that night came from the Scouts Commander of the 101st Airborne Division, Captain Frank Lillyman; *"Special consideration should be given to the 440th and 441st groups of the Troop Carrier Command. Using only radar and no lights because of their uncertain position, forty-seven delivered their personnel to the planned "DZ". This represents more than the other two jump zones combined."*

Randy Hils adds that *"the joy of a job well done, however, had a bitter taste, when news of the fate of the men of the 3rd/506th PIR had been revealed ... Even when the jumps were good, they sometimes went wrong."*

For its missions in Normandy, the 440th Troop Carrier Group won the Distinguished Unit Citation (1).

Frank X. Krebs, who retired from the Air Force with the rank of Colonel, having also been a legislative assistant in the U.S. Senate, died on, May 7 2000 , at his home in Accokeek, Maryland, aged 89. He was born on December 3 1910 in Bethlehem, Pennsylvania to Eva Marie and Frank Krebs. Shortly after his birth, his family moved to Chicago. While still a young man, Krebs took up flying and in 1930 he began his military career by enlisting in the 108th Observation Squadron of the Illinois National Guard. He then worked in aicraft maintenance for U.S. air transport at Camp Midway in Chicago, Illinois. Therefore, he was not only a pilot, but also knew as much as a Crew Chief where his plane was concerned.

He entered active duty as an officer in the U.S. Army Air Corps in November 1939, and after completing his training was assigned to the 1st Squadron of the 10th Transportation Group, based at Patterson Field, Fairfield, Ohio. This unit would later become the initial core of the newly formed Troop Carrier Command. Frank Krebs had activated and controlled the 440th TCG since its inception, leading it successfully through numerous combat missions. Under his leadership, the 440th TCG successfully transported paratroopers and equipment into critical zones during the invasion of the continent. After dropping the 101st Airborne Division in Normandy, Colonel Krebs went with his group to Italy, where he was involved in paratrooper and glider drop missions during the landings in Provence. He had

(1) The Presidential Unit Citation, originally called the Distinguished Unit Citation, is awarded to units of the Armed Forces of the United States and its allies as a reward for heroic conduct during armed conflict.

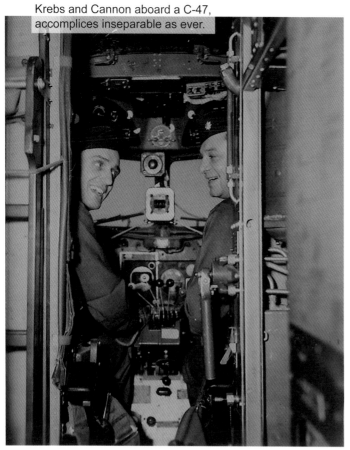

Krebs and Cannon aboard a C-47, accomplices inseparable as ever.

Howard Walter Cannon was born in St. George, Washington County, Utah on January 26, 1912. During World War II he served as a pilot in the U.S. Air Force and was assigned to the European theatre of operations. With Colonel Frank X. Krebs, he participated in the landings in Normandy and Provence, then in the invasion of Holland. He finally retired from the Air Force Reserve with the rank of Brigadier General. For his feats, he received the Silver Star, the Legion of Merit, the Distinguished Flying Cross, the Purple Heart and the Air Medal.

After the war, Cannon became a lawyer and was involved in politics for the Democratic camp. He was Senator for Nevada from 1959 to 1983.
He died in Las Vegas March 6, 2002 aged ninety years.

Frank X. Krebs and Howard Walter Cannon are both buried in Arlington National Cemetery in Virginia.

We will allow Randy Hils to pay tribute to the pilots who transported the troops: "*They were pioneers in airborne assault, special operations and air transport. Their success as combat aviators cannot be evaluated by the number of enemy killed, but rather by the number of lives that they saved, daring to go to war without weapons. The men of the 440th TCG may rightly argue that they have done their duty. Their motto "Nunquam non paratus" (which may be translated as "always ready") continues today with the 440th Airlift Wing of the Air Force Reserve.*"

to rush back to England to drop the 82nd Airborne Division during the invasion of Holland. During Operation Market Garden, Colonel Krebs and his copilot Howard Cannon bailed out of there damaged aircraft. The two men managed to escape the Germans and were able to return to their home base in France forty-five days later. Time and again during tough missions, the experience of Krebs was an advantage to the group and made the difference between success and disaster.

After the war, Colonel Krebs returned to the United States to pursue a career in the Air Force, specialising in training and operations. He retired in June 1965 after 32 years of military service. After leaving the Air Force, he accepted a legislative assistant position along side his former co-pilot and became senator in Nevada. He worked for Howard Cannon for 17 years and retired in 1981. Although he received the Croix de Guerre, Krebs, like many veterans, disliked speaking about these medals.

Daddy Frank with his model A Ford at his home in Accokeek

Reunion of the D-Day Combat Crew in Milwaukee, Wisconsin. The Crew Chief Nagy is missing. From left to right: Sullivan, Arnold, Krebs, Quick, Cannon.

Engaged as a simple private in September 1942, Ed Shames finished his career with the rank of Colonel. An exceptional rise that owes much to his efficiency and bravery in Normandy.

Ed Shames was born on June 13, 1922 in Norfolk, Virginia to a family of Russian origin and Jewish tradition. His father died when he was only 5 years old. Ed started working when very young in order to help his mother who was bringing up four children on her own. From childhood onwards he was imbued with strict principles of education that he held throughout his life: *"Always be the best, be helpful, honest and decent, respect others and make every effort to honour your debts as soon as possible."* After the war he would recount

USA, Fort Bragg, July 1943.

that even at the height of the fighting he always kept up appearances grooming, shaving daily, so that the enemy would know that he was still on top of things.

In 1942, the call to arms reached him from Army general quarters at Fort Monroe, Virginia, where the 506th PIR was assigned. As the country was in need of a shock troop, an elite unit capable of restoring morale after the attack on Pearl Harbour, volunteers were sought with qualities of excellence at all levels. Shames volunteered and enlisted as a private in the 506th PIR on September 1942 at the age of 19.

Seven thousand volunteers presented themselves at Camp Toccoa to pass tests of extreme hardship, from which the best would be selected. Ed was among the 2 500 to 2 800 men finally selected.

Thus, on the night of 5 to 6 June 1944 he was parachuted onto Normandy soil with the men of the 3rd/506th PIR .A member of the company of command in charge of operations, he had previously provided training to all the officers and NCOs of the battalion with the aim of securing two bridges over the Douve, east of Carentan. On the flight to Normandy, Ed Shames would normally

have taken a place alongside Lieutenant Colonel Wolverton, on seat 2. However, shortly before boarding the *Stoy Hora*, Wolverton decided to assign him to another aircraft, probably keeping the seat next to him for a naval artillery observer.

The reasons for this decision were probably many. First, Wolverton needed an observer beside him throughout the operation. In addition, it was preferable that Wolverton and Ed Shames travelled in two different planes, in case the Lieutenant Colonel's aircraft was shot down. Finally, just before

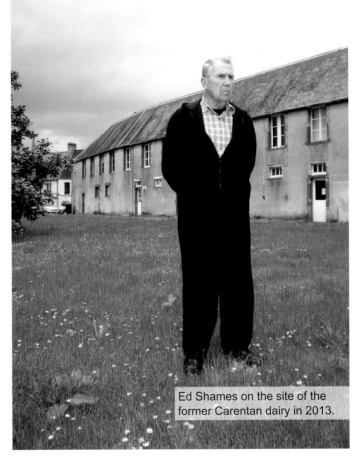
Ed Shames on the site of the former Carentan dairy in 2013.

takeoff, the war reporter, Ward Smith, took the place of the observer.

So by jumping from another aircraft, Ed Shames landed in the town of Carentan, near to the planned location. This did not prevent him from rallying to his objective in the next few hours in the company of just a handful of men.

A few days later, while his regiment was dangerously exposed in a meadow in the Normandy countryside, Ed, whose birthday it was, had a terrible feeling that is epitaph might be, "*Born June 13, died on June 13...*" But, later that day, thanks to his keen sense of observation in the field, his bravery and his spirit of initiative, he made sure that the regimental line of defence was not overrun by German troops. Indeed, it was he who personally undertook to report to his Commander that there was a gap between the companies into which the enemy could infiltrate. In the hours that followed, Colonel Sink, who commanded the regiment, appointed him Sub-Lieutenant.

It should be emphasised that Ed had long dreamed becoming an officer. He enlisted as a simple private and was then moved up the ranks one by one to end up as Chief Warrant Officer. Finally, his dearest dream was realised in the early summer of 1944 when he became the first Non-Commissioned Officer of the regiment to receive a promotion for exemplary conduct on the battlefield.

In September 1944, Shames would take part in the airborne operation Market Garden, most notably in the rescue of a hundred English paratroopers trapped on the right bank of the Rhine after the disaster at Arnhem.

After a brief period in the Haguenau sector in Alsace, he found himself involved in the formidable winter siege at Bastogne in December 1944, where he commanded a platoon of Easy Company, a unit that was to become world famous on account of the *Band of Brothers* book by Stephen Ambrose and its adaptation for the HBO television series. His company can be especially highlighted for its heroic resistance against attacks by German forces during the Battle of the Bulge.

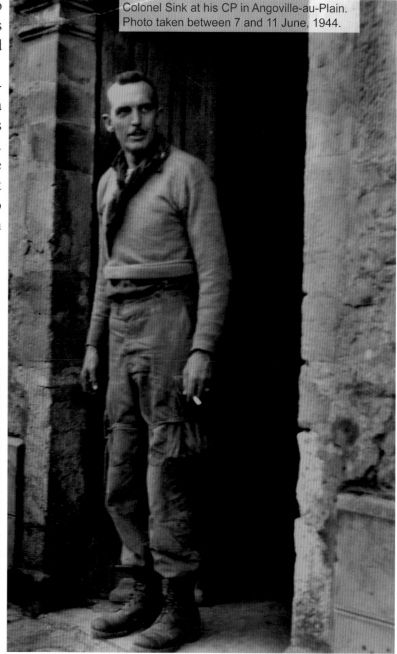

Colonel Sink at his CP in Angoville-au-Plain. Photo taken between 7 and 11 June, 1944.

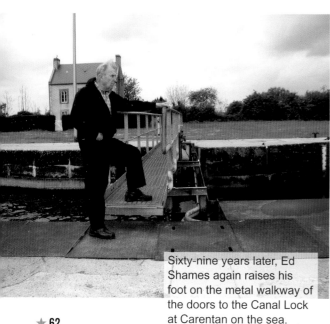

Sixty-nine years later, Ed Shames again raises his foot on the metal walkway of the doors to the Canal Lock at Carentan on the sea.

At the end of the war, Ed was among the first Allied soldiers to liberate the infamous concentration camp of Dachau. Witnessing the monstrosities committed by the Nazis, he did not talk about this until many years later, that is to say in 2012, when finally, for the first time, he agreed to share the discoveries he made there. Marshal Kesselring, who in 1943 and 1944 fought fierce resistance against the Allies during the Italian campaign, personally handed him his revolver when he surrendered.

Throughout his career, Ed Shames had the reputation of being a strict officer, his priority was certainly not to worry about gaining the affection of his men, he simply demanded perfection, and essentially to retain respect. He was highly honoured because of all the units involved, his own recorded the lowest rate of loss from the moment he took command. Moreover, one of his men, while emphasising the harshness of his temperament, paid him this tribute : *"You brought us back home."*

Wounded three times during the war (first in the nose in Normandy, a second time in the left leg in Holland and a thirdly in the back in the Ardennes), he never prided himself on being a hero, preferring to attribute this quality to all the women who had supported them throughout the war by their daily work behind the scenes.

Later, when the *Band of Brothers* book appeared, he agreed to sign the preface with some of his comrades, in order to meet public expectations, while deploring some of the inaccuracies in a few of the stories and the omission to mention numerous soldiers.

After the war, Ed Shames remained in the army and ended his brilliant career with the rank of Colonel. Since then, despite his advanced age, he still regularly attends the veteran meetings of the 506th PIR and various commemorations in Europe. He is married and the father of two boys.

Colonel Shames jokingly confided : *"I would have loved to get the Legion of Honour before dying. I would be as proud as a peacock. I would have liked to have had it, not necessarily for myself but for my family."*

Today he would like to convey this message to future generations : *"Learn as much as possible in the understanding of others, because every person is different. Education is the greatest gift ever accorded mankind. It allows him to understand the manner of the thinking of others, which is as necessarily different from our own as the climates of different countries are different. Peace is a great thing. Man has sought it since the dawn of time. For two thousand years we have tried, but we have failed, apparently we are not strong enough to have found an answer to this dilemma: Will peace have the last word?"*

This photo of Lieutenant Ed Shames, newly found, was taken in London in September 1944 for his girlfriend Ida who was waiting at home in Norfolk, Virginia.

DAHMS THE GERMAN PARATROOPER DREAMS OF THE CINEMA

After graduating from school, Joachim Dahms entered the Film Academy at Babelsberg in Berlin. He wanted to become a cameraman specialising in drama. Unfortunately, the war abruptly interrupted his studies at the age of 20 and he took a much less artistic direction by beginning basic training with the paratroopers.

By the spring of 1944 the young Berliner had joined the Fallschirmjäger - Regiment 6 (FJR.6), an elite unit commanded by Major Friedrich August von der Heydte. In May he arrived in the Cotentin peninsula near Carentan, along with his regiment which numbered 4,100 men, divided into four battalions.

His first encounter with the American paratroopers, who were isolated there, was on the early morning of June 6 near Saint-Côme-du-Mont. That day and the next, Joachim would participate in fierce fighting against the men of the 82nd and 101st Airborne Division supported by the infantry, in the Sainte-Marie-du-Mont sector. For good reason the American paratroopers quickly nicknamed von der Heydtes' soldiers the "Lions of Carentan". Speaking today on the subject of his former opponents Joachim calls them "*my comrades in the 101st Airborne Division.*"

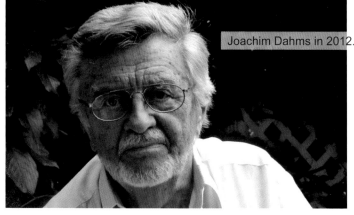

Joachim Dahms in 2012.

The Allies, who undeniably had material superiority, sought without ceasing to push back this particularly pugnacious enemy. In addition to the almost incessantly encroaching combat, the German soldiers found themselves exposed to permanent naval artillery fire courtesy of the battleships cruising off Utah Beach.

Struggling for survival, Joachim experienced the fear of imminent death. During the course of these tragic hours he asked more than once if, immersed in the maddening life or death struggle of war without mercy, he would lose his humanity at the same time as his reason.

The first case of conscience in his life as a soldier came from the desperate cries of very young American soldiers in distress,

At dawn on June 6, Allied ships approach Utah Beach. The naval guns open fire to crush the German position.

who were calling for their mothers. Having received a Christian education, Joachim tried to get closer to God, he prayed intensely to ease his conscience and to seek inner peace.

One day while he was caught up in a dreadful bombardment, he felt an inner peace settle over him in the course of watching an insect crawling laboriously across his fingers. This innocent image, instantly procured in him a deep sense of affection that he has since never forgotten.

The men of his regiment fought until the end, with their will to win intact and an enforced spirit of camaraderie. But during the last days of the fighting, Joachim lost nine of his companions, two of whom he had known since school.

One of his most vivid memories was at Carentan, while the Allies were trying by all possible means to gather their men coming in from the beaches at Utah and Omaha. Overwhelmed by the armoured superiority of the Americans and exhausted by the previous days battles, the Germans felt that they were approaching the limit of their forces.

While wounded by shrapnel, Joachim was taken prisoner and the FJR.6, now bled dry, counted less than a hundred survivors.

Today, American veterans respect and appreciate the loyalty of von der Heydte's fight as they remember his decent behaviour towards the French people during these terrifying days. They have not forgotten how the German officer offered a three hour cease-fire in order to evacuate the wounded and dead. Hating Nazism, von der Heydte was hoping for the collapse of the Third Reich. Joachim still remembers the instructions he gave his men: "*Never shoot anyone who is without defence !*"

During a visit to Normandy during the summer of 2008, Joachim Dahms was warmly welcomed by a French family. Since then, he has visited every year, accompanied by his wife.

A long column of soldiers and American vehicles move towards Sainte-Marie-du-Mont.

German paratrooper nurses identifiable by the armband and the red cross flag, using a Zündapp KS 750 motorcycle.

The Commemorative Steles

The plaque at Angoville-au-Plain.

Angoville-au-Plain

An illustrated panel, placed at the entrance of drop zone "D" commemorated to 3rd/506th PIR Lieutenant Colonel Wolverton. It explains in detail the drop and the action of the paratroopers of the 101st Airborne Division in this sector.

The cross of Méautis, situated at the southern end of the Bloody Gully battlefield, was erected shortly after the war.

The Méautis Cross

This is situated by the side of the road, at the site of the terrible battle of Bloody Gully that raged during the counter-attack of German troops trying to retake the city of Carentan. If the Germans had been victorious, a breach would had been opened between the two beaches, Utah and Omaha. Ed Shames was there that day.

The Magneville Memorial

Just when it was flying across the Normandy coast carrying a group of men from company I of the 3rd/506th PIR, the C-47 No. 2100905 was hit by Flak . In a desperate crash landing, the plane came down in a place called "The Ferage" in the town of Magneville. Every year the 1944 Memorial Association organises a ceremony to the memory of the eighteen paratroopers and four crew members killed at the spot. During this gathering, children from neighbouring schools sing the American national anthem and lay a flowered wreath.

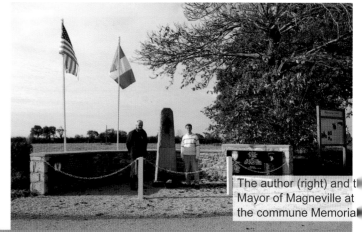

The author (right) and the Mayor of Magneville at the commune Memorial

The Stele at Saint-Côme-du-Mont

Inaugurated in the commune in 2014, in the presence of veterans from the 3rd/506th PIR on the occasion of the 70th anniversary of the landings that also coincides with the 100th anniversary of the birth of Colonel Wolverton, it is placed in the field opposite to the place where he and several of his men lost there lives. On the Stele one can read the prayer that he read to his soldiers before boarding the C-47. A special tribute is paid to the men of the 440th TCG and their leader Colonel Krebs who, as Randy Hils writes : "*From the battlefields of Normandy, across Europe and beyond the Rhine, these were unique among warriors, the fighters without weapons.*"

Simulation showing the Stele of Saint-Côme-du-Mont inaugurated in 2014.
(Drawing : Paul Gros from a photo by Michel Léonard)

The Cemeteries

What a contrast between the American cemetery at Colleville-sur-Mer, with its white crosses perfectly aligned on the lawn, and the German cemetery at La Cambe with its groups of black granite crosses scattered throughout the trees in the park. Officially opened in 1956, the cemetery at Colleville overlooks Omaha Beach. Over an area of seventy hectares, this is ten times larger than the seven-hectares cemetery at La Cambe, and the number of American soldiers buried there is 9383, as opposed to 21,222 German soldiers at La Cambe.

In 1958, La Cambe was the site of the first youth camp organised by the Volksbund in France. Since then , many young volunteers, supervised by the soldiers of the Bundeswehr, have helped to maintain the cemetery.

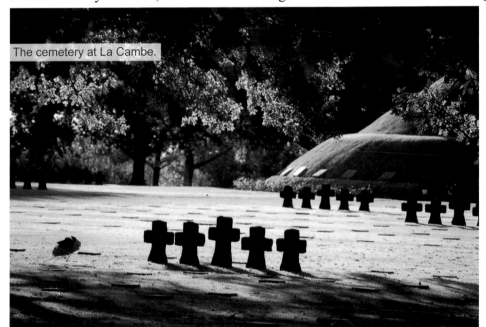

The cemetery at La Cambe.

The most famous grave in the cemetery at Colleville-sur-Mer is that of General Theodore Roosevelt Jr., "Teddy" (1887 - July 2, 1944). Eldest son of the former President of the United States, Theodore Roosevelt and distant cousin of President Franklin D. Roosevelt, "Teddy" commanded the U.S. 4th Infantry Division whose 101st Airborne Division needed to protect the landings on Utah Beach. Felled by a heart attack in the shadow of a Normandy apple tree on July 12 1944 , the General requested that he stay with his compatriots who died in combat.

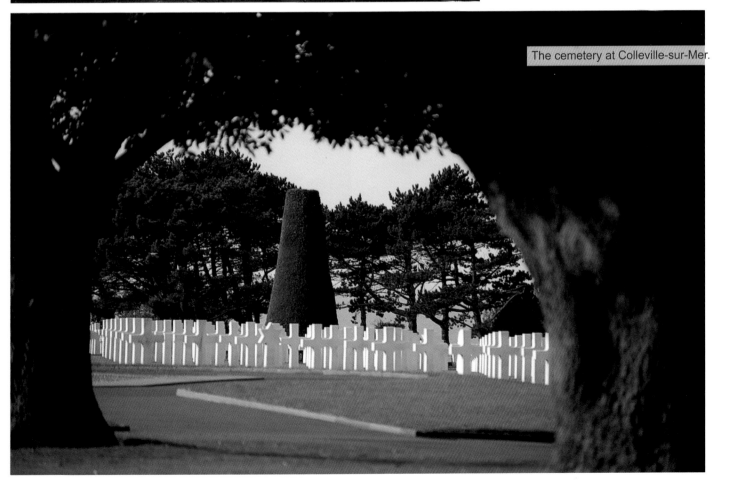

The cemetery at Colleville-sur-Mer.

Carentan - the Bridge at Brévands : in the tracks of Ed Shames

Although it was highly desirable, it has not been possible for me to follow the whole course undertaken by Ed Shames' company prior to the publication of this book. It was therefore with my guide, Michel Léonard, that I followed Ed's path from the place of his drop to the bridge at Brévands. During a second visit with Michael, two years later, accompanied by the designer Christophe Esquerré, I immersed myself for a second time in this historic site that has changed so little since D-Day.

One can easily follow the beginning of the path that Sergeant Shames took to get to the bridge at Brévands. At the moment of jumping, he immediately realised that he was going to land at Carentan, the town he absolutely needed to avoid. In the courtyard of the dairy, his first meeting was with a Normandy cow, the design on a large chimney (since destroyed). Then, under cover of real mooing cows, this time he sprung over the front boundary wall to cross a small bridge next to a brick-makers. Shames then followed the row of trees bordering the canal which were camouflaging German vehicles. He was well advised to avoid this and passed by onto a path on the right. During his progress, he met some stray paratroopers of whom he took command.

After a short stop off in a house, he re-orientated his position thanks to information given to him by a French national astounded by this nocturnal encounter. After crossing one of two metal walkways of the sluice gates near to the caretaker's cottage, Ed crossed the water course by swimming before reaching his objective. Today the bridge no longer exists. Although the site is not accessible to walkers, one can see it from the road alongside the canal.

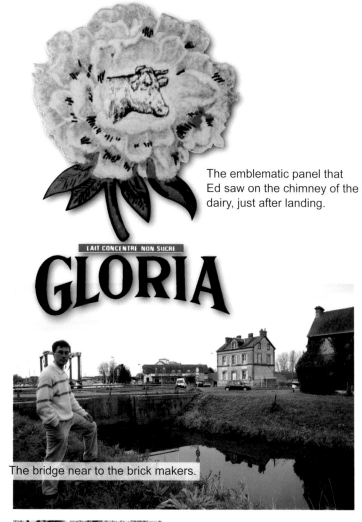

The emblematic panel that Ed saw on the chimney of the dairy, just after landing.

The bridge near to the brick makers.

The row of trees along the canal.

Gilles Vallée by the canal at Carentan on the English Channel, where the river Douve flows.

SAINT-CÔME- DU-MONT,
FIRST FRENCH VILLAGE
"ADOPTED" BY THE U.S.A.

CHAPTER 15

In the spring of 1945, an American named Cecilia Judels made a proposal to the municipality of Saint-Côme-du-Mont "to adopt" the village to help the affected population. A year earlier, her son Robert, a Lieutenant in the 101st Airborne, had landed there in a glider.

During the first millennium of our era, the small Gallo-Roman city suffered both Saxon and Viking invasions. The town was burned to the ground during the Hundred Years War, on July 20 1346 by the soldiers of King Edward III of England. Saint-Côme-du-Mont would not become French again until 1450. In 1815, after the disaster at Waterloo, some thirty thousand Prussians occupied the Channel and coerced the local people into fulfilling their requirements and requisitions. In 1870, after the fall of the Second Empire, the village prepared itself once more for the invading Prussian army, which fortunately did not happen.

Four years had passed since the sad day of German occupation in June 19, 1940. There were just a few hours to go before the landings that were going to change the course of history; a festive air had animated the vicinity. On that Sunday of June 4 1944, the day of the Solemn Communion, the Germans stationed in the town had benefited from some light entertainment at the parish hall. A moment of relaxation before the iron and fire storm...

On the night of June 6, Joe Beyrle, paratrooper with the 3rd/506th PIR landed on the steeple of the church at Saint-Côme.

He then jumped into the cemetery and headed towards Rue Mary, but he was wounded and then taken prisoner. Joe Beyrle died Dec. 12, 2004 . In 2005, his son Joseph later erected a plaque right at the spot where Joe touched down on Norman soil.

On Tuesday, June 6 at dawn, Lieutenant-Colonel von der Heydte, commander of the FJ. Regt 6, climbed up into the belfry of the church to overview the general situation. In view

The hamlet of Basse-Addeville, destroyed by the bombings that took place during the night of 7 to 8 June 1944.

of the spectacle spread out before him, he decided to move his command post to Saint-Côme and started to move his regiment.

In the early afternoon, while crossing the Quincy, the artillery of the FJ. Regt 6 column of American paratroopers, silenced enemy positions established at Saint-Côme by bombarding them with 150 mm shells.

Michel Godefroy the first civilian victim at Saint-Côme, died on June 6 at 18:00 hours. The next day, Marcel Lepaisant was shot by the occupying troops. He had mistakenly been suspected of helping the Allies by sending them signals, though he was only laying out tarpaulin, rather unwisely. During the night of 7 to 8 June, the tower was destroyed after five hours of bombardment by German artillery who did not want the Allies to use it as an observation post. It collapsed shortly after 7am. That same day, Odette Letourneur, 25, and Georgette Revet, a little 8 years old girl were killed near the road bridge at Pénême. Further along, a bombardment had destroyed the village of Basse-Addeville, killing ten people of which six were children. During the course of that tragic night, the Langeard family paid a very heavy price for the war. The parents died with four of their children aged 5 to 12 years old. Paul Langeard was the only sibling to survive. Seriously injured, he was treated by the Americans in the church at Angoville-au -Plain.

June 8 at 4:45 hours in the morning, the 101st Airborne stormed Saint-Côme. Colonel Sink and Colonel Johnson established their CP in a house at a place called "L'Amont" at the intersection of the Route Nationale 13 and the road to Sainte-Marie-du -Mont (On June 6, 2005, the Paratroopers Historical Centre, devoted to the history of the 101st Airborne, was established in this house). June 8 in the evening, after four long years of occupation, Saint-Côme was finally liberated.

On 11 November 1948 the French Secretary of State for the army awarded the Croix de Guerre with a bronze star to Saint-Côme, "a village, two-thirds of which had *been ravaged and whose population accepted this sacrifice with courage and selflessness."*

Gustave Laurence was the mayor of Saint-Côme from 1941 to 1947 and municipal councillor until 1953, and the mayor once again from 1959 until his death in 1962. A member of the Resistance, wounded three times and cited twice for his exploits during the 1914-18 war, he had been decorated with the Croix de Guerre, the Grande Guerre medal, the Médaille de la Victoire and the Médaille Militaire. However, all through his life he sought to keep silent concerning his activities during the Second World War.

On April 22 1945, nearly a year after D-Day , Gustave Laurence was surprised to receive this letter from the American, Cecilia Judels :

"Our committee has the intention of adopting your village, with the purpose of repairing it in accordance with the American government. Please give us your answer.
Sincerely.
Cecilia Judels
New York, April 22, 1945
Norman Village Reconstruction Committee" (1)

Cecilia Judels had good reason for wanting to help the people of Saint-Côme-du-Mont. Having lived in France with her family, she had learned to know and love this country and she modestly wished to help restore its greatness. In addition to this, her son Robert, a Lieutenant in the 101st Airborne Division, had been in one of the first gliders to land on the night of 5 to 6 June 1944.

Used on a grand scale for the first time in a conflict, gliders had played a central role in the success of D-Day. At the time they were the only way of transporting the equipment needed by the Airborne Divisions to fight and push forward : ammunition, food, Jeeps, small calibre guns, but also reinforcements. On D-Day

This embroidery, found amongst Cecilia Judels' artefacts', was returned to the Saint-Côme town council after her death.

and D-Day +1, more than four thousand men were thus sent to the heart of the battle in 512 gliders.

Gustave Laurence responded positively to this offer, which manifested in the establishment of a genuine Marshall Plan on the scale of a Normandy commune. And Saint-Côme-du-Mont thus became the first French village to be adopted by the Americans. The first emergency packets arrived in October 1945. Hence 120 kilos of soap, coffee, chocolate, sugar, quinine and 200 dollars (10,000 francs at the time) of relief were distributed to the victims and the sick.

The 547 inhabitants of the village, to which were added refugees, received clothes, shoes and wool to repair their clothes. Later, the school was able to reopen thanks to specific donations. People also received food and regular medical assistance. The population showed its gratitude to its godmother in various ways. The children sent her drawings, residents despatched foodstuffs to her while living in Paris as she was subject to post-war rationing.

Finally, the town officially decorated Cecilia Judels, American benefactor of Saint-Côme-du-Mont.

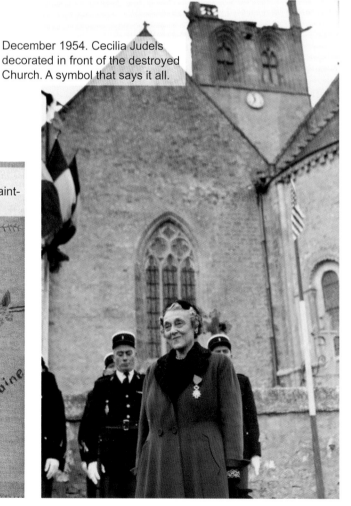

December 1954. Cecilia Judels decorated in front of the destroyed Church. A symbol that says it all.

(1) In the book *Saint-Come-du-Mont : Témoins d'hier (Yesterday's Witnesses)*, one can see the emotional correspondence between Cecilia Judels and Gustave Laurence as well as the full history of the church, classified under the title Historical Monument.

Three museums dedicated to D-Day are located in the Utah Beach area, presenting a wide variety of uniforms, weapons and vehicles as well as numerous models staging life-size scenes. Archival films permit a full discovery of the faces of the D-Day protagonists.

The Utah Beach D-Day Museum

In 1962, Michel de Vallavieille, then mayor of Sainte-Marie-du-Mont, decided to create a memorial to express his gratitude towards the American soldiers.

Built on a German bunker, this museum is composed of more than 3,000 m² of space, exhibiting a rich collection of objects on two levels, including vehicles and equipment. A vast semi- circular room offers a spectacular view of Utah Beach where the men of the U.S. 4th Infantry Division landed. The story of the battle is illustrated by a chronological sequence that recounts in ten sequences the events of D-Day from preparation through to completion.

The film *The Beach and the Victory*, which was awarded the CINE Golden Eagle Award for documentary in 2012 and the Special Jury Prize in 2013, revives the epic story of the soldiers engaged in the largest amphibious operation of all time, thanks to exceptional archive images enriched by very realistic visual effects.

Renovated in 2011, the building has been expanded into a specially designed hall to accommodate the "star" of the museum, an American B-26 Marauder bomber. There are only three models of this aircraft existing worldwide, in itself one of the keys to the Allied victory in Normandy.

Musée du Débarquement Utah Beach
50480 Sainte Marie du Mont
Tél. : 02.33.71.53.35
E-mail : musee@utah-beach.com

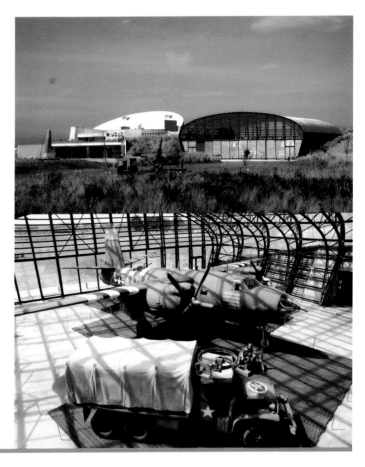

The D-Day Paratrooper Historical Centre at Saint-Côme-du-Mont

Born out of the passion of a Belgian historian, Michel De Trez and the Normandy born Emmanuel Allain, opened in June 2005 this museum is situated at the entrance of the village of Saint-Côme-du-Mont in the house that served as a former command post for Lieutenant-Colonel von der Heydte's, FJ. Regt 6 German paratroopers before being used successively as a German infirmary, as a U.S. infantry base, and finally as a command post for U.S. paratroopers.

In front of this museum of sixty years before, the American and German troops battled very hard on 7 and 8 June for control of the crossroads route (RN 13 Paris -

Cherbourg) connecting the town of Carentan to Utah Beach. The exhibition showcases extremely realistic models, fully equipped with weapons and equipment from the epoch.

Internationally recognised specialists, Michel De Trez and Emmanuel Allain contribute regularly to numerous historical military publications. They often collaborate for film and television projects, most notably on Steven Spielberg's film *Saving Private Ryan* and the no less famous *Band of Brothers* series.

Dead Man's Corner Museum
2, Village de l'Amont
50500 Saint-Côme-du-Mont
Tél. : 02.33.42.00.42
E-mail : carentan.101@orange.fr

Airborne Museum, Sainte-Mère-Eglise

Located in the heart of Sainte-Mère-Eglise, this museum is entirely dedicated to American paratroopers, and leads the visitor through the battles fought by the men of the 82nd and 101st Airborne Division during the night of 5 to 6 June 1944.

Both buildings shaped like a parachute canopy, are separated by a park which displays vintage vehicles. Unique aspects of the museum include, in the interior of the first building, the exhibition of a model of a Waco CG-4A glider, unique in France.

In the second building there is a re-enactment of the boarding of the 3rd/506th PIR by paratroopers from the 101st Airborne, and an authentic Douglas C-47 D-Day Skytrain, all filmed by a cameraman of the Army Signal Corps. Among the paratroopers with blackened faces mingle a few men sporting Indian war face paint and the crests of the Iroquois. They belong to the section known as the "Filthy Thirteen" of the 506th Regimental Headquarters Company 's demolition platoon.

The first building of the extension was inaugurated in 2014 for the 70th anniversary of D-Day.

Musée Airborne
14, rue Eisenhower
50480 Sainte-Mère-Eglise
Tél. : 02.33.41.41.35
E-mail : accueil@ airborne-museum.org

APPENDICES

How did this book come into being?

It all began in 1984 in my school library, with the discovery of a photograph illustrating the book The Longest Day by Cornelius Ryan. I spent hours studying it, asking myself a thousand and one questions, minutely observing the American paratroopers until they became familiar to me.

It was at this point that my desire was born to come and visit the beaches of the landings. In 2010, during a trip to Normandy with my teenage son and two of his friends, I discovered the book Tonight We Die As Men by Ian Gardner and Roger Day. I got in touch with Ian, who quickly introduced me to Michel Léonard, Deputy Mayor of Saint-Côme-du-Mont and translator of his book. Thanks to this providential assistance, my understanding of events became refined. I embarked on a thorough study of it. It was a revelation and the starting point for my work.

My curiosity unsatisfied, I undertook historical research that allowed me to make friends in Europe and the United States.

On my way I met Christine Krebs Goyer, eldest daughter of the commander of the 440th TCG, responsible for the aerial transport of the 3rd/506th PIR on D-Day. Her availability and attention to my project allowed me to summarise the involvement of the 440th from the beginning of World War II until the landings with the help of the writings of Charles Everett Bullard, Veteran of the 440th TCG and Randy Hils, a historian whose father served with the 440th TCG.

It is my hope that my work will serve to perpetuate the memory of those brave young men who, through the personal sacrifice of their lives, participated in the great momentum of liberation in Europe.

My desire to see their story illustrated in colour has been born through this book.

Gilles Vallée

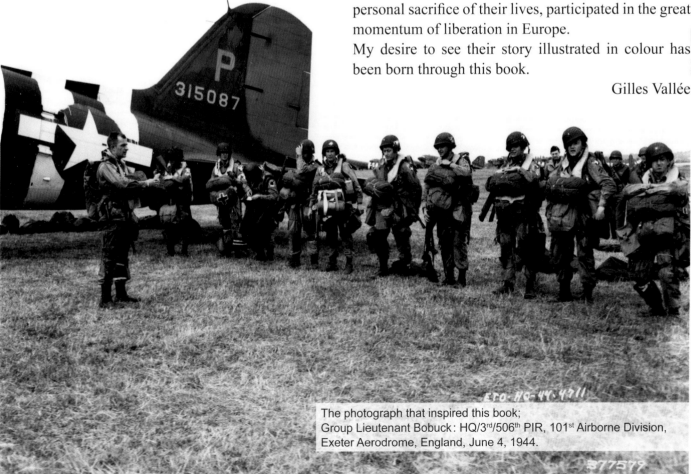

The photograph that inspired this book;
Group Lieutenant Bobuck: HQ/3rd/506th PIR, 101st Airborne Division,
Exeter Aerodrome, England, June 4, 1944.

Secrets of the men of the 440ᵗʰ TCG

After the Great Depression of the 1930s, many young Americans longed to escape from a mediocre present and a future that promised little better. They therefore conceived the desire of enlisting in the army. Charles Everett Bullard himself was not at all keen to help on the family farm.

Charles Everett Bullard during the war.

One day, while watching a magnificent large aircraft, he became determined to join the Air Force. Having successfully passed the stringent physical and mental aptitude tests, he proudly won his first badge, convinced that his childhood was behind him. Thus he joined the 440ᵗʰ Troop Carrier Group. This unit counted among its ranks some of the best pilots in the U.S. Air Force, united by their common love of aviation and their passion for flying.

Each unit of the 440ᵗʰ was personalised by a design placed on her nose called Nose Art. This mystery regarding the *Stoy Hora* is explained to us by Randy Hils: "*The mystery has hung around for a long time. For what reason was Colonel Krebs' aircraft, the 42-92717, named the Stoy Hora and why did the Nose Art alongside the name on the nose of the aircraft representing a caricature of a Ringmaster with a moustache shaped like a bicycle handlebar and dressed in top hat and tails, display the words Stoy Hora? There were in the 440ᵗʰ TCG some Spanish speaking artists who had composed the drawings on the nose of the aircraft. The name comes from a slang expression in Spanish "Estoy ahora". Estoy: "I am" and Ahora: "here now". Literally: "I'm here now for you. "*
Based on these observations, I conclude that it was a code that indicated the aircraft Commander."

Christine Krebs Goyer says her father, Frank X. Krebs, while he was at Wright Patterson before the war, met her mother while she was studying art at the Dayton Art Institute. Paul and Emily Agnew became close friends with Mr and Mrs Krebs before the war. Paul, who was in the 440ᵗʰ TCG during the war, had created the Nose Art for the *Miss Yank*. John Agnew, a professional

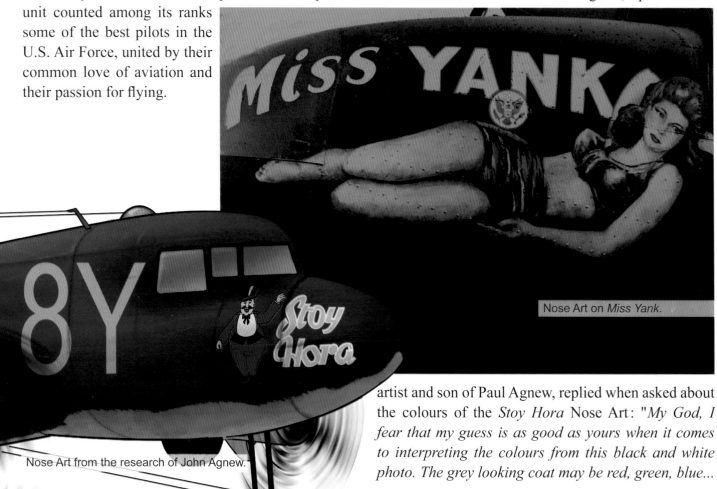

Nose Art on *Miss Yank*.

Nose Art from the research of John Agnew.

artist and son of Paul Agnew, replied when asked about the colours of the *Stoy Hora* Nose Art: "*My God, I fear that my guess is as good as yours when it comes to interpreting the colours from this black and white photo. The grey looking coat may be red, green, blue...*

who knows? I guess the Nose Art artists mixed their colours from an ensemble of primary coloured paints, so that the colours should not be anything too exotic. I would say you should make your best estimate, and if there is nobody to challenge your proposition, then it may be that. This is how history is often written! If I had to guess, my choice would be a red base coat with yellow or blue letters."

The work of Charles Everett Bullard is teeming with a multitude of details that create emotional richness and authenticity in his testimony. He writes about his memories of the war: *"As far as I am concerned, with rare exceptions, these months have been among the most valuable of my life."* At the end of his book, while thinking about his children and grandchildren, he concludes with a reference to the Nose Art on his plane: *"These charming, lovely people, and many others all over the American continent, should be aware that all these facilities that they take for granted today would not be available to them if men and women, just like those of the 440th, had not made all these sacrifices during these years when the freedom of the world was at stake. In reality, without the presence of my "guardian angel" none of them could have been here today."*

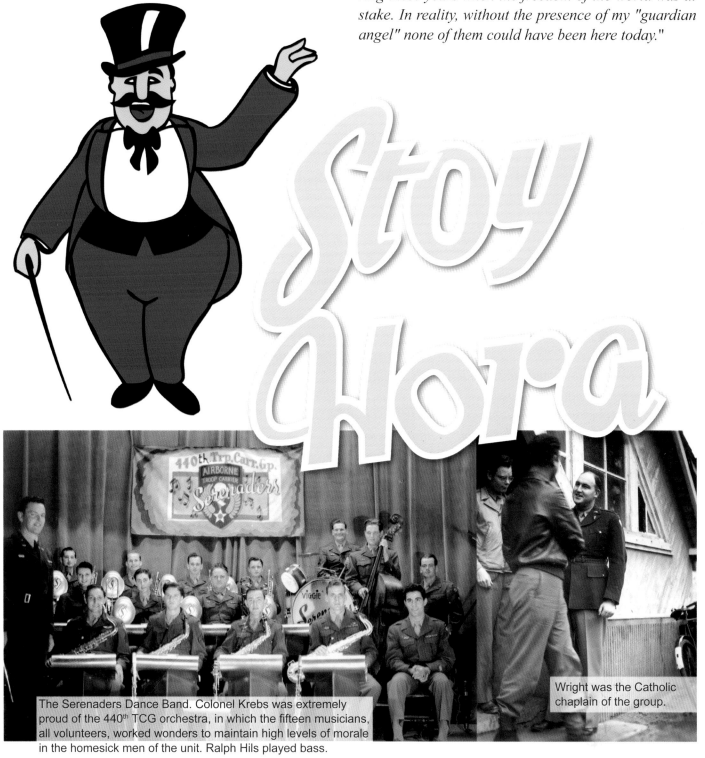

The Serenaders Dance Band. Colonel Krebs was extremely proud of the 440th TCG orchestra, in which the fifteen musicians, all volunteers, worked wonders to maintain high levels of morale in the homesick men of the unit. Ralph Hils played bass.

Wright was the Catholic chaplain of the group.

Ed Shames' Homage to Robert Wolverton

Wolverton was undoubtedly one of the most admirable officers in the history of the United States. He was an exceptional human being. He could manage his own officers just as well as the volunteers, and he made it very easy. I think this was an innate quality, because I do not think he learned this at West Point.

I was with him almost every day, every hour of the day, and during the long hours he confided in me. He trusted me and I was very grateful.

He was absolutely crazy about parachute jumping. He loved jumping off planes, while I hated it! But I went with him all the same. Every time he walked past an airstrip, he tried to convince me that he needed to try to see if he could pull off a little jump! And I was obliged to follow him!

Everyone expected to die. Among those I worked with, and all of those with whom I had made friends, none of them expected to return home. Of course we wanted to, fervently, but if you're a good soldier, you are finally ready to give your life for your cause. Wolverton certainly always had this thought in mind. It was his destiny! He was born to be not only a great leader, but also to be an exceptional person. He was someone who had an enormous amount of culture, and it is terrible to think that he never touched French soil while assigned to France.

For my part, I just did my job and I tried to accomplish it as well as possible because I was a perfectionist. I am very proud of two things: The first was when I received the first Battlefield Commission (1) of the 101st Airborne Division (after Normandy) and the second when I brought home more men in my section than any other regimental division. However, this is not because we did not do much in the war! I was in the third section of the company E as an officer. We had been chosen by Colonel Sink to be the patrol section of the regiment. In other words, they needed some information while we were on the battlefield, and they asked my section to provide this information when we placed ourselves behind the German lines. And despite all that, I brought home more men than all the other sections! I was not personally responsible for this achievement. It was primarily because I was extremely strict towards my men in teaching them all that they were able to learn before starting a mission. It was a question of survival. I was known as being a very hard and difficult man. But I was hard because I wanted to be sure, to be certain, that I was doing everything in my power to bring my men home. My men did not like me until the moment I returned them to their homes after the war!

I think I was a good soldier, but I have trained men who became better soldiers than me.

Colonel Shames

(Interview by Henriette Wiehe, during a telephone conversation with Colonel Shames in December 2012)

(1) Promotion to a rank of officer of an NCO who has shown evidence an exceptional ability to command on the battlefield

TABLE OF CONTENTS

p.3   Introduction. **Robert Lee Wolverton and Frank Xavier Krebs**

p.4   **1. Eisenhower worries for his paratroopers**

p.7   **2. The Prayer of Lieutenant Colonel Wolverton**

p.9   **3. The 3rd Battalion of the 506th Regiment**

p.12 **4. Equipment and weapons of the U.S. paratroopers in Normandy**

p.22 **5. At Exeter aerodrome, 4 and 5 June 1944**

p.28 **6. The Douglas C-47 "Stoy Hora" and its crew**

p.32 **7. The 440th Troop Carrier Group**

p.36 **8. On board the "Stoy Hora"**

p.43 **9. "I saw them jump to destiny"**

p.52 **10. What happened to Lieutenant Bobuck's Men ?**

p.58 **11. What became of the crew of the "Stoy Hora" ?**

p.61 **12. The meteoric rise of soldier Shames**

p.64 **13. Dahms the German paratrooper dreams of the cinema**

p.66 **14. In the footsteps of the D-Day Participants**

p.69 **15. Saint-Côme-du-Mont, first French village "adopted" by the U.S.A.**

p.71 **16. Visiting museums in the Utah Beach area**

p.73 Annexes. **How did this book coming into being ? / Secrets of the men of the 440th TCG / Ed Shames' Homage to Robert Wolverton**

p.78 Glossary

p.79 Thanks

p.80 Documentary resources and photographic credits

GLOSSARY

G.I : Government Issue or General Infantry, common name given to the soldiers of the U.S. Army.

US VII CORPS : 7th Corps of the American Army, including the U.S. 4th Infantry Division, the 82nd Airborne Division and the 101st Airborne Division.

506th PIR (PARACHUTE INFANTRY REGIMENT) : 506th Parachute Infantry Regiment of the 101st Airborne Division.

3rd/506th PIR : 3rd Battalion, 506th PIR.

HQ/3rd/506th PIR : Command Company headquarters of the 3rd/506th PIR.

326th AIRBORNE ENGINEER BATTALION : 326th Airborne Engineer Battalion of the 101st Airborne Division.

327th GIR (GLIDER INFANTRY REGIMENT) : 327th Infantry Regiment transported by gliders belonging to the 101st Airborne Division.

IX AIR FORCE : 9th U.S. Air Force comprising the IX TCC (Troop Carrier Command).

50th TCW (TROOP CARRIER WING) : Unit IX TCC, consisting of the 439th, 440th, 441st and 442nd TCG .

440th TCG (TROOP CARRIER GROUP) : 440th Transport Group Troops consisting of 95th, 96th, 97th, 98th TCS .

98th TCS (TROOP CARRIER SQUADRON) : 98th Squadron of the 440th TCG .

SERIAL : Ensemble specifically composed of four or five groups of nine C-47 aircraft

CREW-CHIEF : Crew member responsible for the aircraft and passengers.

F.J. REGT 6 : 6th German Parachute Division.

MARSHALL PLAN : American Plan to assist in the reconstruction of Europe after World War II .

VOLKSBUND : German Association working towards the upkeep of German war graves in 45 countries.

THANKS

My sincere thanks to Christine Krebs Goyer, Nicole Laurence, Michel Léonard and Ian Gardner, as well as to the veterens Ed Shames, Charles Everett Bullard and Joachim Dahms for their confidence and amicable encouragement, and for their help throughout the implementation this book.

My deep gratitude to Henriette Wiehe and the Designer Christophe Esquerré for their commitment to my side and the immense work they have accomplished with enthusiasm and generosity over many months.

Three crucial people joined us in the final phase. Without them , this book would not be what it is. I want to mention Jean-Charles Stasi, Chief Project Coordinator of the team, as well as Paul Gros and Charles Henry Groult who have deployed their artistic talent to make this documentary-book a work destined for the widest possible audience.

I also thank Jérôme Delile from "L'Aure du Commun", Bayeux, for his informed study of the drawings of planes and paratroopers; Philippe Trombetta for his help and expert advice; Esvelin Philippe, Jean Laurent, Dominique Potier and Xavier Van Daele who kindly shared valuable information on the men of HQ/3rd/506th PIR.

I wish to pay tribute to George Bernage, Founder of Editions Heimdal, and its Director, Ghislain Cheguillaume. Through their confidence and tenacity, both have made the realisation of my project possible.

I would also like to thank the following people for their hospitality, their availability and their help: Pierre Fauvel, Mayor of Saint-Côme-du-Mont, Maurice Duchemin Mayor of Magneville; Emmanuel Allain and Michel De Trez, Co-directors of the D-Day Paratrooper Historical Centre at Saint-Come-du -Mont, Ingrid Anquetil, Director of the Utah Beach D-Day Museum; Magali Mallet, Director of the Airborne Museum at Sainte-Mère-Eglise, his Technical Assistants Eric Belloc and John Vervalle; The American Battle Monuments Commission and staff-member Anaëlle Ferrand; The Association of Notre-Dame-des-Ailes and its President Jean Michel; The Association of the 506th Airborne Infantry Regiment and its Adminstrator Kevin Kilkenny; The IKLK France (Cercle International Karl Leisner) and its President Aloyse Rimlinger; News International Syndication, London, and staff-member Sarah King; George Theis of the Troop Carrier Association and the Glider Pilot Association.

My gratitude goes to John Agnew, Frederic Bonnelais, Hans den Brok, Thérèse Dieudonné born Jacquet, Mark Durivage, Christophe Eudeline, Patrick Frappier, Lajos Jambor, Anne -Marie Laufer, Anne -Christine Loubignac, Regis Maubry, Evangel of Jesus, Monica Perin, Jean-Pierre and Solange Ruozi.

A big thank you to Martine and Michel Léonard, who warmly welcomed me at their charming guest house in Saint-Côme-Du-Mont, the "Clos Sajot" in the immediate vicinity of the landing beaches.

Thanks, finally, to all those that I may have forgotten.

DOCUMENTARY RESOURCES AND PHOTOGRAPHIC CREDITS

Bibliography

American Warriors, pictorial history of the American paratroopers prior to Normandy, Michel de Trez, D-Day Publishing, 1994

Atlas du débarquement et de la bataille de Normandie 6 juin - 24 août 1944, John Man, éditions Autrement, 1994

Bataille de Normandie, (coll. « guides Gallimard ») éditions Les Nouveaux-Loisirs, 2004

DZ EUROPE, The Story of the 440th Troop Carrier Group, Mark Durivage, 2012

Fighting with the Filthy Thirteen, Jack Womer et Stephen C. Devito, Casemate Publishers, 2012

Histoire des opérations aéroportées, éditions Elsevier Séquoia, 1979

Karl Leisner - Victor in vinculis (Vainqueur dans les chaînes), Bande dessinée parue aux éditions Coccinelle, 2011

La 101st Airborne Division dans la Seconde Guerre mondiale, Vanguard of the Crusade, Mark Bando, Heimdal, 2012

Les paras du D-Day, Christophe Deschodt et Laurent Rouger, éditions Histoire et Collections, 2004

Little One And His Guardian Angel, Charles Everett Bullard, éditions Williams Associates, 2001

Magneville ce jour-là... 6 juin 1944, Philippe R. Nekrassoff et Eric Brissard

« Nunquam Non Paratus Never Unprepared The 440th Troop Carrier Group in Operation Neptune », Randolph J. Hils, in *Airborne Quarterly Magazine*, winter 2003, p.55-61

Order of Battle, Operation Overlord, Utah Beach and the US Airborne Divisions, 6 June 1944, James Arnold et Roberta Wiener, Ravelin Limited, 1994

Saint-Côme-du-Mont : Témoins d'hier, Michel Léonard et Nicole Laurence, préfacé par Rémy Villand (directeur-adjoint des Archives départementales de la Manche de 1964 à 2007), (coll. « Inédits et introuvables du patrimoine normand ») éditions Eurocibles, 2005

The Filthy Thirteen, Richard Killblane et Jack Mac Niece, Casemate, 2003

« The Invaders : Wings over Normandy », Randy Hils, article non publié

The way we were N°3 - DOC Mc Ilvoy and his parachuting medics WWII paratroopers, portrait de Michel de Trez, D-Day Publishing, 2004

Tonight We Die As Men, Ian Gardner et Roger Day, éditions Osprey, 2009

Sitography

Ed Shames:
http://www.usairborne.be/Biographie/biographie_us.htm
Men of the 506th PIR :
(*The 506th Airborne, Infantry Regiment Association*)
http://506infantry.org/
(*Find a Grave*)
http://www.findagrave.com/
Archives NARA :
http://www.archives.gov/

Filmography

Band Of Brothers, Home Box Office, A division of Time Warner Entertainment Company, 2002

The Longest Day, Darryl F. Zanuck, Productions Inc et Twentieth Century Fox Film Corporation, 1962

Les guerriers de la nuit, Michel De Trez et Jean-Michel Selles, D-Day Publishing, 1994

The Forgotten Battalion, Whizz Films, 2009

Front cover: Signal Corps - Centre Historique des Parachutistes du Jour-J, Saint-Côme-du-Mont | flyleaf and 1.: Paul Gros | 3. Top: Christine Krebs Goyer / Bot: courtesy of M. Bando collection, via Lee Wolverton | 4.,6.: NARA | 9. Top: Collection Philippe Trombetta / Centre: Ian Gardner / Bot: Robert Webb, Jr., fils de Robert Webb, Sr. HQ/3/506 | 10.: Crown Copyright 1944/MOD, reproduit avec la permission du Controller of Her Majesty's Stationery Office. Remerciement spécial à l'Air photo Archive at Keele University, Staffordshire - collection de Ian Gardner | 12-18.: Centre Historique des Parachutistes du Jour-J, Saint-Côme-du-Mont - American Warriors, pictorial history of the American paratroopers prior to Normandy (except 12. Bot: collection particulière / 13. Centre R: Signal Corps - Centre Historique des Parachutistes du Jour-J, Saint-Côme-du-Mont / 17. Top L: US Army, Signal Corps) | 19. Top and 20. Top L: Signal Corps - Centre Historique des Parachutistes du Jour-J, Saint-Côme-du-Mont | 20. Centre: Gilles Vallée / Bot: John Reeder - Centre Historique des Parachutistes du Jour-J, Saint-Côme-du-Mont | 21.: Centre Historique des Parachutistes du Jour-J, Saint-Côme-du-Mont - American Warriors, pictorial history of the American paratroopers prior to Normandy | 22-26. Signal Corps - Centre Historique des Parachutistes du Jour-J, Saint-Côme-du-Mont (except 26. Bot and 27: Signal Corps - Christine Krebs Goyer) | 28. Top and 29.: Christine Krebs Goyer / Bot: Gilles Vallée | 31. Top: Christine Krebs Goyer / Bot: Signal Corps - Centre Historique des Parachutistes du Jour-J, Saint-Côme-du-Mont | 32.: Collection Philippe Trombetta | 33.et 35. Top: Christine Krebs Goyer | 42. 52. Bot and 53. Top: Robert Webb, Jr., fils de Robert Webb, Sr. HQ/3/506 | 52.-57.: Signal Corps - Centre Historique des Parachutistes du Jour-J, Saint-Côme-du-Mont (except 52. (Legion of Merit) : The way we were N°3- DOC Mc Ilvoy and his parachuting medics, WWII paratroopers, portrait Michel de Trez, D-Day Publishing, 2004 / 53. (Harrison): Robert Webb, Jr., fils de Robert Webb, Sr. HQ/3/506 / 53. (Wolverton): Signal Corps - Christine Krebs Goyer / 55. (Bobuck): John Reeder - Centre Historique des Parachutistes du Jour-J, Saint-Côme-du-Mont / 54. Bot, 56. Bot and 57.Top R: ECPAD - Ian Gardner) | 58.: Gilles Vallée | 60.: Christine Krebs Goyer | 61. Top: Robert Webb, Jr., fils de Robert Webb, Sr. HQ/3/506 | 61. and 62. Bot : Ian Gardner | 62. Bot: John Reeder photo, via M. Bando collection | 63.: Ed Shames - Ian Gardner | 64. Top: Joachim Dahms / Bot: Coll. Musée d'Utah Beach | 65. Top: D.F.-Heimdal / Bot: Bundesarchiv | 66. and 67.: Gilles Vallée | 68.:Gilles Vallée (except Top: Michel Léonard) | 69. and 70.: Saint-Côme-du-Mont – Témoins d'hier, Nicole Laurence et Michel Léonard, préfacé par Rémy Villand, (coll. « Inédits et introuvables du patrimoine normand ») éditions Eurocibles, 2005 | 71.: Musée du débarquement d'Utah Beach | 72. Top L: Centre Historique des Parachutistes du Jour-J, Saint-Côme-du-Mont / Top R and Bot: Gilles Vallée | 73.: Signal Corps - Centre Historique des Parachutistes du Jour-J, Saint-Côme-du-Mont | 74. Top L: *Little One And His Guardian Angel*, Charles Everett Bullard, éditions Williams Associates, 2001 / Bot R: Collection de John Agnew, fils de Paul Agnew - Christine Krebs Goyer | 75. Bot L: Collection de John Agnew, fils de Paul Agnew / Bot R: Christine Krebs Goyer | back cover: (patches) Collection Philippe Trombetta / (photo) Signal Corps - Centre Historique des Parachutistes du Jour-J, Saint-Côme-du-Mont

Achevé d'imprimer en avril 2014 sur les presses d'OZGraf à Olsztyn (Pologne) pour le compte des Éditions Heimdal